# PEACE FOR OUR PLANET

## A New Approach

# ROYA AKHAVAN, PH.D.

Wisdom
Editions

Minneapolis

Wisdom
Editions
Minneapolis

FIRST EDITION JANUARY 2017
PEACE FOR OUR PLANET: A New Approach
Copyright © 2017 by Roya Akhavan

Printed in the United States of America.
10 9 8 7 6 5 4 3 2 1

Cover and interior design: Gary Lindberg

ISBN: 978-1-939548-64-1

# PEACE FOR OUR PLANET

## A New Approach

# ROYA AKHAVAN, PH.D.

For my grandfather, Dr. H.N. Javdan, who showed me
what it means to be a true human being.

# Table of Contents

# Introduction

There is a new positive energy of enormous power stirring in the world, and it is leading us to a new way of life; one that is more peaceful and just. This may appear to be a counter-intuitive statement, given what is most visible to the naked eye. For thousands of years the history of humanity has been an unfolding drama of horrible and great suffering for the majority of the people who inhabit the earth, and the turmoil continues. A few hours of watching the news or reading about the current state of international affairs is enough to create deep concern, sadness and even hopelessness. To anyone who has not yet become desensitized to the bloody scenes of violence perpetrated by terrorists or numbed by the deadly corruption of divided governments, the trajectory of our world appears to bend toward growing destruction and disintegration.

These processes of destruction and disintegration are quite real. There is no doubt about that. But another equally profound and real process is unfolding alongside the destructive process; one of constructive integration. Although less visible to the casual everyday glance, it is a reality that is moving forward in the world, parallel to the destructive process, and it can be seen quite clearly when examined from a historical perspective.

This bifurcation—the parallel movement of the constructive alongside the destructive—became greatly pronounced in the middle of the nineteenth century. Coinciding with the sending of the first telegram in 1844, which in itself brought down the barriers of time and space, almost all charts of human activity, whether in the scientific or the social realm, began to move from a nearly horizontal to a nearly vertical position. This is clearly visible, for example, in the chart showing the number of inventions patented in the United States. For hundreds of years, the line showed little upward movement. Then, starting around 1850, it suddenly made a sharp turn toward exponential growth. Another clear example, this one from the social realm, is the upward swing of the number of laws passed against slavery across the globe. In both the scientific and the social realms, humanity began to show signs of a highly accelerated movement away from barbarism toward civilization.

This constructive movement in the direction of a more civilized world has not yet attained its ultimate goal; there is still much work that remains to be done. And yet, it is a process that cannot be stopped. Nor can it be turned back.

This book is an attempt to make visible and bring into focus the constructive processes of unification and integration moving forward in the world alongside the self-destruction that is going on in the realms of the old and the outworn. It is also an attempt to depict the new dialectic within which the constructive ideals challenge the destructive process, while the horrors of the destructive process energize and give new momentum to the constructive process.

As I will show in this book, the future of the integrative process is bright. However, we must still work to facilitate and accelerate its movement. We must also work to soften the effects of the crash-landing of the outworn behaviors and institutions as they go through their death pangs and collapse within the destructive realm.

As we come to recognize the contours of the integrative process in our world, we must also develop the personal consciousness required to align ourselves with the energies that are being generated by it. It is primarily through such a personal alignment with the integrative spirit of our age that we can become catalysts in its advancement and mitigate the suffering that the destructive process continues to inflict upon millions of people around the world.

This book is organized into five parts:

1.  In view of the hopelessness that the many ills of our world have generated in people's hearts and

minds, and given the growing disenchantment with the existing political institutions that appear to be incapable of resolving even their own intra-party conflicts, it is imperative that we first talk about reasons for hope. Is there any hope for the future of humanity? And if we are saying that there is indeed hope, then what are the empirical evidences and logical arguments that can support such a bold assertion?

Confidence in the possibility of achieving peace is the most important ingredient in setting out on a journey to explore and participate in a new approach. For that reason, the first part of this book will focus on providing concrete evidence of the integrative processes that have been going on in the world during the last two centuries. I will attempt to show that, despite the blinding haze and fog created by the accelerated collapse of outworn behaviors, systems and institutions, there really is a steady process of resilient growth moving humanity in the right direction.

2. The second chapter will explore the unprecedented dialectic within which the acceleration of the constructive process since the nineteenth century has challenged and threatened the primary elements of the destructive process that comprise the root causes of war (i.e., racism, nationalism, religious strife, gender inequality and extremes of wealth and poverty).

3. In the third chapter, we will discuss the relationships between these root causes of war and the phe-

nomenon of terrorism as a case study of how these destructive elements manifest themselves in this rapidly growing threat to security around the globe. We will also explore the reasons why traditional approaches to combating terrorism have proven so ineffective.

4.  The fourth chapter will further elaborate on the reasons for the failure of traditional approaches to maintaining security, including direct military intervention and/or engineering of a balance of military power by global superpowers. These approaches belong to the destructive plane and have become completely ineffective in the twenty-first century.

5.  The last part of the book will be dedicated to delineating a new approach to peace and presenting solutions at both the systemic and individual levels. We will make tangible and intimate connections between our lives as individual inhabitants of the planet and the larger integrative processes going on in the world and discuss the constructive concepts that have already taken root at the systemic level but need our individual contributions to grow and bear fruit.

# Part 1: The Constructive Process

As already stated, even in the context of a critical analysis of the complex social, political and economic challenges facing contemporary global society, two key clarifying concepts can provide us with a hopeful vision for the future of humanity. One of these is the recognition of a major shift in global consciousness put into motion by the transformative scientific and spiritual discoveries that began in the mid-nineteenth century. The other is the onward march of two parallel historical processes; one of destruction and the other of construction.

Most of us do not need an account of the evidence of the disintegrative process at work in the world today. We see it in the growing specter of terrorism, the ongoing regional wars, an unprecedented refugee crisis, the bloody clashes among people of various races, religions and ideologies and the persistence of poverty, racism and sexism, just to name a few.

In the upcoming chapters, we will turn our attention to a deeper analysis of these destructive processes. The aim of this chapter, however, is to depict the constructive process so that we can pursue our new approach to peace with a realistic expectation that the attainment of a lasting peace is not only possible, it is inevitable; and that the primary choice facing humanity today is whether peace is to be achieved through a process of consultation and collaboration or realized only after a violent destabilization of the planet by a harsh crash-landing of outworn mindsets and institutions.

In this book, the constructive process refers to the workings and effects of the positive energies that are moving the nations of the world toward collaborating with each other based on the recognition of universal human rights and the dignity of all people. The ultimate destination of this constructive process is a world in which racial, religious and national prejudices have been eliminated and a lasting peace has been realized. The destructive process, on the other hand, refers to the disintegration associated with the outworn modes of individual thought and institutionalized behavior that no longer meet the needs of a global community, but continue to put up a bloody fight to maintain themselves. Authoritarian, patriarchal, xenophobic, racist, ultra-nationalistic, religiously extremist and other outworn systems that are currently experiencing their death-pangs are the primary actors in this destructive process.

Given the sharp contrast between the two visions to be analyzed in this book—one of disintegration and collapse and the other of advancement toward an ideal civilization—a question arises that must be answered: Is this vision of a peaceful world merely a utopia and a result of pious hopes and dreams, or is it an achievable goal? And if we are saying that it is, indeed, an achievable goal, what are the empirical and scientific evidences and logical arguments that can provide us with a foundation for hope?

A surprising fact of life in the twenty-first century is that empirical evidences of a positive and accelerating trend toward a better world abound in historical data. There are large numbers of quantitative charts and graphs available on the internet, all of which depict the same positive historical trends. One of the richest sources of such data can be found in the work of Max Roser at www.ourworldindata.com.

It is extremely important to point out that assessing progress does not, in any way, mean that the work toward achieving any of the ideals to be discussed in this book is finished. An extensive discussion regarding the unfinished work that still remains to be done will follow in the upcoming chapters.

It is also important to acknowledge that, at times, the turmoil in the destructive plane may lead us to believe that progress has been lost or that conditions have worsened in one or more of these arenas. This tendency, which creates anger and hopelessness, makes it all the more important to understand the robustness of the constructive process and the fact that it is indeed moving forward, unhindered, on its own plane. In fact, the accelerated turmoil in our world today may, in large part, be considered to be the result of the threat posed by the constructive process to the destructive; not the other way around.

Thus, the aim of this chapter is to set the stage for hope by making the constructive trends of the last two centuries visible in brief outline.

One of the things that we notice immediately upon looking at historical trends during the last two hundred years is that revolutionary movements began to take place in every aspect of human life in the early to mid-nineteenth century. The most obvious of these was the exponential rise in the number of scientific discoveries and technological innovations. But, more importantly, many other new and historically unprecedented civilizing trends also started during the same period.

One of these trends was the emerging awareness of equality of rights for all human beings. Visible movement in the area of recognition of human rights started in the 1800s with a sharp rise in the number of laws enacted against slavery, the abolition of which took great sacrifice on the part of many courageous human beings, including those who fought to eradicate the practice in the United States. This unmistakable trend in the rise of the legitimacy of enlightened ideals, not only in the United States but also around the world, ultimately led to the adoption of the Universal Declaration of Human Rights in 1948, which today constitutes a cornerstone of international law.

In addition to the increasing recognition of universal human rights, another example of the positive progress in the constructive plane is reflected in the Human Development Index—an index consisting of life expectancy, literacy, education and GDP growth. Throughout the last century, there has been a steady upward trend toward literacy, health, life expectancy and economic growth around the world.

Another positive trend, essential to the topic of this book, is the decrease in violence and war deaths. During the nineteenth century, the French Revolutionary Wars killed seventy out of every hundred thousand people. In the twentieth century, despite two world wars and a few genocides, the average number of war deaths went down to sixty out of one hundred thousand worldwide. So far in the twenty-first century, the worldwide average of the number of deaths caused by war is down dramatically, to 0.3 per hundred thousand.

During the last several decades, many scholars have noticed the decline of war and violence around the world and have written about it. For the purposes of this book, I will focus on the work done by Steven Pinker, a professor of psychology at Harvard University. Pinker's voluminous book, published in 2011, is entitled *The Better Angels of Our Nature: Why Violence Has Declined*. As the name suggests, this book documents the decline of violence in our world and the loss of legitimacy, not only of war, but also of all forms of violence in the collective international culture.

Pinker reminds us that just a few centuries ago, invading other countries and conquering them was a normal part of the job description for every national leader. During the last several decades, however, invasion for the purpose of territorial expansion has not only gradually disappeared from the pages of history, it has become illegal under international law.

Despite the fact that civil wars still continue to rage in some parts of the world, during the last forty years many significant transformative events have happened in the direction of a more peaceful world. Just four decades ago, we lived in a world in which any of the following changes appeared hopelessly impossible. Yet, all of them took place in succession and within a relatively short period of time.

1. The Soviet Union and the United States declared peace in the early 1990s, officially ending the Cold War, which had made the threat of a nuclear conflagration a part of every child and adult's daily experience. The Iron Curtain in Europe was torn down, and the former Soviet republics became independent states.

2. China abandoned the extreme ways of the Cultural Revolution after the death of Mao and began its peaceful rise under Deng Xiao Ping, becoming a major trading partner to the United States and the rest of the world within the short span of two decades.

3. Apartheid, one of the most blatant forms of institutionalized racism, was dismantled in South Africa,

and the white minority peacefully transferred its political power to the black majority.

4. Fascism and dictatorship began to wane as primary modes of government, giving way to liberal democracy in countries that had gone from one military coup to another for decades, among which we can name Portugal, Spain, Greece, Taiwan, South Korea and many other countries in South and Central America. There were fewer than twenty democracies in the world in 1976. Today, that number has increased to over one hundred.

5. Most remarkably, Europe, which had given the world two of its bloodiest wars as recently as the first half of the twentieth century, found its way to peaceful cooperation. This process first began with the formation of a multilateral economic collaboration within the European Coal and Steel Community, which then expanded to become the European Economic Community, and finally gave birth to the European Union, complete with its own European Parliament and laws, the European court and a common currency. The borders between these countries, which had seen so much bloodshed for centuries, are now marked by nothing more than a welcome sign.

6. It is important to note that, during the last few decades, similar arrangements have developed in South America (UNASUR), Southeast Asia (ASEAN) and Africa (AU). Regional economic and political unions, which include plans for the elimination of

formal border checks and adoption of common cur-rencies, are on the rise across the globe.

7. The world saw an end to the process of colonial-ization, with formal political independence of all for-mer colonies by the 1970s. Although the destructive trend continues in the form of neo-colonial practices, the two categories of imperial war, to gain sovereign-ty and to keep it, no longer exist.

But to just speak about these trends with data is not enough. A scientific discussion needs both the data on the patterns and trends and a logical explana-tion that would only be possible if we can pinpoint the cause of these transformative trends. In other words, once we have seen this data the question be-comes: What is/are the cause(s) for these dramatic shifts and changes?

Pinker tries to explain these patterns of reduc-tion in violence through their association with oth-er civilizing trends, such as increases in literacy, IQ and economic interdependence, all of which have also moved in a positive direction. In essence, Pinker offers the Kantian explanation that our human rea-son, combined with the rational desire to preserve our self-interest, has led us from the lower aspects of our nature toward the "Better Angels of Our Nature," namely, self-control, empathy and cooperation.

However, this reasoning is not able to explain why human beings started becoming visibly more literate, intelligent and rational in the nineteenth century and what has been the cause of the accelerating momentum toward the advancement of civilization.

In response to this question, we can put forward the thesis here that the source of these changes has been the discovery of new spiritual truths during a heretofore largely unacknowledged period of enlightenment in the nineteenth century.

Just as there are physical laws and formulas in science, there are also spiritual laws and formulas that are equally as precise and powerful as the physical ones. When scientists discovered physical laws, such as magnetism or electricity, or when Einstein discovered $E=MC^2$, they discovered truths that had always existed, but until that moment of discovery we had remained oblivious to them. Scientific discovery of a cause and effect relationship, for example, means taking the veil away from a physical truth that had always existed, but we were not previously able to see or understand it.

Once a physical truth is discovered, it unavoidably spreads throughout the world. Different people are inspired by it and enabled to advance it to the next level; to use it to innovate new things that did not exist in the world before. In other words, the discovery of new truths is always followed by new inventions based on that discovery.

It was the discovery of new physical truths, and the innovations based on them, that has been the source of the accelerating processes of technological change during the last two centuries, enabling us to turn silicon, which is elemental sand, into a means of communication with distant planets.

In the same way, the nineteenth century saw the discovery of major spiritual truths that humanity was previously oblivious to:

1. The earth is one country and humankind its citizens.

2. Women and men have been created equal.

3. There is only one race—the human race.

Just like the newly discovered physical truths, these spiritual truths had always existed, but until the veil was removed from them they were absent from the collective consciousness of humanity.

The discovery of these ideas set into motion an unprecedented process of positive social change, which, though slow and gradual, has been moving steadily and decisively in the right direction.

The first stirrings of action toward the concept of women's liberation that went beyond limited philosophical discussions happened with two events coinciding in close historical succession in the summer of 1848. Surprisingly, the first of these events happened in one of the darkest spots on earth as it related to any recognition of rights for women, namely at a conference held in Badasht, Iran, with the participation of one woman and eighty men who had gathered to discuss the fate of a new revolutionary movement (the Babi movement). During that conference, Tahirih, a famous poet and courageous leader within the movement, removed the veil from her face as a symbolic act of removing the veil from the promise of a new world for all of humanity. Within days of that historic event, another decisive step was taken at the Seneca Falls conference in New York, where Elizabeth Cady Stanton and her compatriots passed a declaration on the need to advance the rights of women, including the then very radical idea of voting rights for women.

Another innovation during that same period was the rapid rise in the number of peace societies. The number of these societies multiplied to four hundred from the middle to the end of the nineteenth century.

The nineteenth century also marked the first time in human history that the idea of peaceful coexistence among nations went beyond being a topic of discussion among thinkers and philosophers to become an idea discussed by the world's political leaders. In 1899, Tsar Nicholas II of Russia convened the first international conference of the world's sovereigns in The Hague to discuss a means for the peaceful settlement of disputes. The most tangible product of that conference was the establishment of a panel of experts in international law that could offer help in resolving international conflicts. Regardless of the judgment of history about Tsar Nicholas II, the significance of the seed planted by the mere elevation of this idea to the realm of political discussion is undeniable in view of the events that followed it.

Not long after that conference, the destructive process in the world led to the outbreak of WWI. It was the horrific shock of that bloodshed that propelled the world's leaders to take steps to strengthen the constructive innovation that had taken place in The Hague two decades earlier. This time, the Treaty of Versailles in 1919 (which itself was full of contradictions and imperfections) contained a provision for the establishment of a Permanent Court of International Justice and the world's first formally organized intergovernmental body, the League of Nations, which was established in 1920. Although the league collapsed within two years, it provided an important precedent for the coming together of the world's nations within a collective system.

Once again, within a decade, the destructive processes in the world led to the Second World War. But this time, the magnitude of the destruction and bloodshed stimulated the resolve of the international community to establish a far more comprehensive system of supranational cooperation (i.e., the United Nations).

Thus, half a century after the first intergovernmental gathering at The Hague, the ideas discussed at that conference came to full fruition; first with the establishment of the World Court as an integral part of the United Nations, and then fifty years after that, with the establishment of the International Criminal Court (ICC), both of which are now headquartered at The Hague and are empowered to enforce international law, with the World Court hearing cases against nations and the ICC having the jurisdiction to prosecute individual leaders of nations for crimes against humanity.

Another unprecedented innovation, reflecting the awakening of collaborative impulses, was the increasing engagement of the civil society through non-governmental organizations (NGOs) in furthering human rights and sustainable economic development. Since 1948, these global NGOs have functioned as two-way networks between the United Nations and the civil society, providing insights about local realities and collaborating with relevant bodies in the UN system to implement global objectives in peace-building, environmental sustainability, healthcare, education and human rights.

The maturation of the constructive collective consciousness throughout the twentieth century enabled a long list of international conferences to be held under the auspices of the United Nations, bringing together representatives from governments and the civil society to address a wide range of issues vital to the progress and prosperity of humanity as a whole. Some of the most visible successes of this accelerating process of international collaboration have come about since the Millennium Summit of the United Nations, held in September 2000, which brought together heads of state and high-ranking officials from 189 countries. The Millennium Declaration adopted by these global representatives included a series of new "Millennium Development Goals," in the context of which the delegates committed their nations to collaborate with their global partners to, 1) eradicate extreme poverty and hunger, 2) achieve universal primary education, 3) promote gender equality and empower women, 4) reduce child mortality, 5) improve maternal health, 6) combat HIV/AIDS, malaria and other diseases, 7) ensure environmental sustainability and 8) develop a global partnership for development. A major sign of this growing global commitment to action was the adoption of measurable time-bound goals, to be achieved by 2015 and updated at regular intervals.

Another unprecedented milestone, reflecting the maturation of the global integrative consciousness, was the 2015 Paris agreement on preserving the environment, in the context of which representatives from 196 nations marked the first time in history that all sovereign countries in the world had agreed on, and committed to, a path forward toward comprehensive action to curb climate change and protect the planet.

Building on the momentum demonstrated in Paris, the first World Humanitarian Summit was held in May 2016 under the auspices of the United Nations, with the theme of "One Humanity: Shared Responsibility," in Istanbul, Turkey. The aim of the summit was to underscore the need to prepare for and provide effective and unified humanitarian assistance to innocent people across the globe that are displaced by conflict and war. In the context of a "New Agenda for Humanity," the world's leaders from 153 countries committed themselves to stand behind their "responsibilities to the world's people," based on the recognition that delivering on those responsibilities "is a moral imperative and a strategic necessity." The summit called for a "major shift in how the global community prevents suffering by putting humanity at the heart of global decision-making."

Another innovation reflecting the operation of a maturing constructive global consciousness is the intergovernmental collaboration within the United Nations in support of a multinational deployed police force, namely, the United Nations international peacekeeping forces. This process started with sending unarmed blue berets into various hot spots in the world as observers to help keep the peace. Over the last few decades, the UN peacekeeping forces have evolved and are now allowed to carry and use arms to protect themselves and others. As of 2015, the UN peacekeeping forces represented the largest deployed military body in the world, with 125,000 peacekeepers from 128 countries. Through their missions, these peacekeeping forces have been remarkably effective in reducing the chances of sliding back into war, with an expenditure that accounts for less than 1 percent of the world's military budget.

Another innovative process of transformation that began in the late nineteenth century was the birth of the interfaith movement in 1893, when representatives from Christian, Muslim, Jewish, Hindu, and

Buddhist faith traditions came together in Chicago to engage in an unprecedented dialogue. The exponential growth of the interfaith movement within the span of a century was exemplified in the depth and breadth of the Parliament of World Religions held in the United States in October 2015, which represented people of fifty different faith traditions from eighty countries who had come together in a common mission "to cultivate harmony among the world's religions and spiritual communities and foster their engagement with the world and its guiding institutions in order to achieve a just, peaceful and sustainable world."

Another innovation, which has shown visible growth in the twenty-first century, is the rapid expansion of involvement by major businesses in philanthropic efforts and projects, aimed at promoting socio-economic development across the globe. This approach is driven in large part by the demands of a growing body of younger consumers, including the millennials in the United States, who are the most socially connected and globally conscious generation of all time. The number of businesses that link their commercial activities to global ethical concerns has risen exponentially, in line with the new orientation displayed by the millennials.

In addition, for the first time in human history, the world's richest people are personally engaged in spending their vast resources to improve the lives of the less fortunate across the globe. The growing consciousness among the rich about their responsibility to help heal the planet and its people is manifested by such billionaires as Bill and Melinda Gates and Warren Buffet, who have persuaded 150 of their billionaire counterparts to join them in signing the "Pledge" to give away 50 percent of their wealth for the betterment of the world. These collective positive intentions find new synergies when coupled with the availability of unprecedented scientific knowledge and talent that can provide ethical, accessible and environmentally friendly technological solutions to some of the most pressing problems facing underdeveloped communities.

Finally, during the last few decades, the academic world has embraced the field of peace studies as a discipline in its own right. The rapid growth in peace studies is a further reflection of the growing collective consciousness about the need to achieve peace. Less than half a century ago, only a handful of universities in the United States offered programs of any kind in this field. Today, the number of such universities has grown to more than one hundred, with forty universities offering full-fledged undergraduate degrees in peace studies and many providing opportunities for advanced degrees.

Thus, we can conclude that, as of the twenty-first century, the constructive consciousness of our age has converged in a growing acceptance of a shared responsibility to serve the collective interests of humanity. The innovative nature of this unprecedented transformation becomes clear when we consider that, until a century ago, the history of human civilization was shaped by a worldwide culture that consistently glorified division, supremacy-seeking and warfare. Can these unprecedented innovations be the result of anything other than the discovery of new spiritual truths?

Even in this brief discussion we can see clearly that, in the last two centuries, every horrific event in the destructive plane has fueled the constructive process in an unprecedented dialectic. In this new dialectic, the processes of destruction and construction do not clash with one another; rather, they move forward, simultaneously and side-by-side, on separate planes. These two processes are related only in the sense that each destructive event creates an initial shock and turmoil that, instead of in any way reversing humanity's progress, gives new energy and fuel to the constructive process.

In addition, in this new dialectic, both of these parallel movements are irreversible. Once an old system has been abolished, efforts to reestablish it, however forceful and bloody—or temporarily successful—are doomed to ultimate failure. And, by the same token, once a new evolutionary constructive trend has been put into motion, it will continue to move forward in the world. It cannot be stopped, nor can it be turned back.

Why is it then, we might ask, that at this juncture in human history the destructive process in the world is so much more visible to the naked eye? This glaring visibility is the result of the fact that the destructive process and the outworn mindsets associated with it have been challenged under the spotlight shone on them by the constructive process. In response, they have resurfaced in the most extremist form, in a last flare.

As such, contemporary extremism, whether political or religious, may be viewed primarily as a reaction to the threat presented by the new spirit of the age to an outworn and dying way of life, be it: religious extremists seeking to reestablish caliphates and revive Sharia law in the Middle East; white supremacist groups spreading hate against immigrants and identifying them as the root of all social ills in various western countries; or political candidates promising to return a country to its old days of glory. All of these entities share a striking similarity. They all look to the old days as their utopia and hold out the promise to their desperate listeners that *they* are the ones who will succeed in turning back the clock to the days when pride and privilege were bestowed upon them simply because they belonged to a specific group.

Although capable of prolonging havoc and destruction, these reactionary movements represent the last gasps of a dying order. The urgent, and yet hopeful, message of this book is that, as co-creators of our own destiny and that of other human beings, each of us has the power to align ourselves with the positive energies and integrative processes that are inherent in the spirit of our age. As such, we are able to become powerful catalysts in facilitating the constructive process and mitigating the prolongation of the suffering being meted out by the ongoing death pangs of the destructive order.

# Part 2: The New Dialectic

Up until the nineteenth century, the history of humanity was characterized by a relatively slow crawl by the human race toward incorporating various civilizing influences. In the mid-nineteenth century, however, this civilizing process suddenly branched into a separate, energetic, rapid and unstoppable movement that has since begun to challenge, and even threaten, the destructive patterns of social life and political organization that had retained their legitimacy throughout millennia.

At the time this challenge began in the nineteenth century, many destructive mindsets and behaviors were still at the height of their legitimacy around the world. Stronger countries colonized the weaker ones, wealthy individuals legally owned their fellow human beings as slaves and men treated women as part of their personal possessions. Even in the most advanced democratic countries, women lacked many rights, including the right to vote. Up until the nineteenth century, there was no shame in any of these modes of behavior. Indeed, all of them were upheld as morally justified and even necessary, reflecting the natural order of things. Physical force, military or otherwise, reigned supreme. "Othering" and separation, supremacy-seeking, domination through assertion of power over others by self-aggrandizing dictators and death of innocent soldiers and civilians in service to the schemes of their leaders; these comprised the basic elements of life in most human societies across the globe. The primacy of domination through exertion of physical force also perpetuated the subjugation of women and emboldened, to the extreme, the glorification of all things "masculine." Economic exploitation of others, supported by material greed, at both the systemic and the individual levels, combined with the discrimination and deprivation experienced by people of certain races and countries, created and maintained large gaps between the haves and have-nots, perpetually resupplying the tinder-box for instability and war.

The common genesis of all of these destructive elements was the success of demagoguery; that is, the use of a particular physical characteristic or social construct by power-mongers and supremacy-seekers to divide human beings, dehumanize and create fear of the "other" and convince those who got to identify themselves as belonging to the "insider" circle to give their lives to ensure the perpetuation of the power of their leaders. These structures of domination and subjugation, fueled by myths of insider superiority and outsider inferiority, became so reified and internalized that their existence appeared natural and God-given. As such, they gave rise to a powerful hegemonic hold on the common human beings' psyche, despite the fact that they spawned unspeakable misery among those who were subjugated and a harmful perversion of spirit within those who were "privileged" by them.

All of these processes are still going on in the twenty-first century within the destructive realm. The key point, however, is that, unlike two centuries ago, when they represented the natural order, they have now been delegitimized. Under the light of the constructive ideals that have gained momentum in the world, the hideousness of these destructive mindsets has been increasingly revealed. Today, racists, sexists and fascists can no longer stand up with pride and assert their destructive views with impunity. They will be called out and delegitimized.

Precisely because of this constructive collective consciousness, which has come to challenge and, indeed, threaten outworn mindsets and worldviews, upheavals of various kinds have developed within the destructive plane; those who have lost legitimacy and privilege will not give up their familiar and comfortable ways without a fight. They are bound to take a last stand.

In light of the constructive ideals toward which humanity is evolving, we are now able to recognize more clearly than ever the immoral and senseless nature of the destructive factors that have comprised the root causes of misery and war throughout human history—namely, racism, nationalism, religious strife, inequality of women and men and extremes of wealth and poverty. While these forces still remain part and parcel of the destructive plane and continue to affect the lives of the vast majority of people around the globe, it is clear that they have begun to unravel and collapse under their own weight in the twenty-first century.

As these destructive constructs and the institutionalized modes of social and political organization associated with them go through their death pangs, turbulence and turmoil is unavoidable. As co-creators of our own destiny, however, each of us has a choice at this critical historical juncture. We can get caught up in the destructive process, or we can work to accelerate the constructive process. There is great reason for hope that by working within the constructive plane, and by gently beckoning and accompanying others to join us, the level of destabilization and suffering that is bound to result from the inevitable collapse within the destructive plane will be greatly mitigated.

In this chapter, we will examine the new dialectic of the last two centuries and the nature of the challenges posed by the constructive process to the destructive elements that have caused so much misery for humankind throughout millennia.

## Racism

Throughout the centuries, racism was a root cause of war both within and among nations. It gave rise to unjust relationships of domination and oppression among various races and set into motion a vicious cycle of discrimination, hopelessness and poverty for millions of people across the globe.

The devastating consequences of racism continue to play out within the destructive plane to this day. Yet, remarkably, one of the most egregious manifestations of racial subjugation, namely slavery, was among the first social ills to be addressed during the nineteenth century, leading to an exponential rise in the number of laws enacted internationally against slavery and, ultimately, to the abolition of the practice in Britain and the United States.

Indeed, viewed in a historical context, the rapid acceleration of the challenge that began in the United States during the nineteenth century to a destructive social order characterized by slave ownership is a remarkable testament to the power and resilience of the constructive process. Inspired and guided by the spirit of the new age, President Abraham Lincoln stood up as the first political leader in the United States to present a forceful challenge to a social order built on the backs of African slaves. There is no need here to recount the story of the Civil War that led to the abolition of slavery in the United States. What is important to point out, however, is that the ultimate triumph of the Union over the Confederate Army showed that, even in the nineteenth century, people who were willing to sacrifice their lives to uphold justice had greater strength and spirit than those who clung to their quest for wealth through enslavement of other human beings.

Yet, despite the abolition of slavery, a growing collective consciousness about human rights and a steady march toward delegitimization of racism throughout the world, progress toward eliminating racial prejudice remained painfully slow. During the twentieth century, in particular, a number of political leaders were tragically successful in fanning the flames of racial prejudice against various ethnicities by pointing the finger at them as scapegoats for their nation's problems.

It is painfully clear, for example, that the extreme racism of Hitler and his ability to persuade the vast majority of German people to join his quest for making the Aryan race "the lord of the earth," was a major cause of the world's bloodiest and most devastating war in all of history, leading to the death of over fifty million people across the globe, including a Holocaust during which six million Jewish people were rounded up and brutally killed in concentration camps.

Half a century later, the rise of political leaders in the former Yugoslavia bent on exploiting ethnic identity to gain power, such as Slobodan Milosevic who later came to be known as the "Butcher of the

Baltics," led to bloody conflicts among the Serbs, Croatians, Bosnians, Slovenians and Albanians, leading to unspeakable misery for millions and the deaths of more than two hundred thousand people.

Concurrent with the ethnic strife in the former Yugoslavia during the closing decade of the twentieth century, the 1994 genocide in Rwanda—rooted in a Belgian colonial divide-and-conquer tactic that had historically given the people of Tutsi ethnicity preference over the Hutus—ended in the slaughter of eight hundred thousand Tutsis at the hands of the Hutus in the short span of one hundred days. The conflict between the two groups subsequently spilled over to other countries in the region and long remained a quagmire on the African continent.

Another ethnically-rooted tragedy is the oppression of non-Arabs (the majority of the population) in Darfur by Sudan's Arab President Al-Bashir that has led to the death or displacement of millions of non-Arabs in a process identified as an ongoing genocide by the International Criminal Court.

In the United States, the legal changes against slavery stopped the most egregious form of institutionalized subjugation of blacks. However, it did little to eliminate racism from people's hearts. With every new challenge to its hateful precepts, the destructive process responded with lynching, systematic racial segregation and Jim Crow laws.

In the context of the new dialectic of history, however, these reactions within the destructive plane soon energized the civil rights movement under the leadership of Martin Luther King Jr. and his many other black and white compatriots and supporters, leading to a major leap forward in the constructive process. Within the span of decades, the forward march of this constructive process made it possible for the people in the United States to elect a black president for the first time in American history.

Once again, the challenge posed to the destructive plane by that historic event shook the structures of white supremacy to the core and gave rise to a "birther" movement and spewing of the most hateful racially motivated rhetoric against President Barak Obama. Nevertheless, the constructive process continued to move forward. There were enough hearts changed in the United States to make it possible for the first black president to be reelected for a second term, despite the strident efforts of those in the destructive realm.

While racism still continues to operate within the destructive plane in the twenty-first century, it has been identified, called out and delegitimized. The delegitimization of racism under the influence of the constructive process has happened gradually and often goes unnoticed by the people who are most affected by it, perhaps because of the utterly exhausting pain of being on the receiving end of racial injustice. The institutionalized dimensions of the legacy of slavery in the United States, for example, have wreaked such profound havoc in the lives of so many black people by perpetuating poverty, unsafe housing, mass incarceration and alienation of a large number of young black males, that much work still remains to be done at all levels to reduce its devastating effects.

Yet, there is little doubt that the constructive process continues to pose a growing challenge to the destructive mindset that is racism. A recent manifestation of this dialectic in the United States has been the growing collective consciousness about the on-going vestiges of segregation and racism reflected in the plight of black citizens in their encounters with the police. New technologies have become an ally of this rising consciousness, and hidden practices that used to go on in the dark are now being exposed by instant videotaping on smartphones.

Following a recent string of deaths involving innocent black men (and women) during investigations of minor offenses and the retaliatory ambush and killing of innocent police officers, new conversations have started among the policymakers and the public, in the mainstream media and through social media to address institutionalized racism, restore mutual trust between the police and the communities they serve and end the destructive stereotyping of young black men and police officers alike. Many deep-rooted and festering racial issues have bubbled to the surface and are being expressed and discussed openly for the first time. Once again, in this ongoing conversation, the voices of the allies of the oppressed are much more audible and effective than the loud and strident shouts of those who continue to cling to their outworn and delegitimized views. As a result, more people are realizing the false dichotomy of pitting "blue lives" against "black lives," the importance of recognizing institutional racism and providing appropriate training to police officers and the need to join forces to build mutual trust. Despite the unfinished struggle for racial justice, the emerging constructive collective consciousness against racism has brought the dire consequences of racial prejudice to light and delegitimized its existence.

## Nationalism

For many centuries, the primary unit of human identity across the globe consisted of tribal affiliation. Sometime around 500 AD, however, the boundaries of this primary unit of identity expanded from the tribe to the nation. The unification of the diverse and warring tribes of Arabia under the banner of Islam provides one of the earliest and most striking examples of this shift.

This newly expanded unit of human identity, however, did not remain immune to the recurring social dynamic of "othering." Soon, the familiar notions of in-group exclusivity emerged in a new form (i.e., nationalism). In its most destructive form, nationalism came to represent a state of extreme psychological attachment that perverted a natural love of homeland into an instrument of hate and disdain for other countries and peoples. It caused a state of mind in which conquest over other countries was seen as the destiny of the nation, and the soil of one's country appeared, at times in far more than a symbolic sense, as truly sacred and of superior quality to the soil that covers the rest of the planet. The extremes of nationalistic delusion often went beyond thinking that one's country is right, to reach a complete state of blind devotion reflected in such expressions as "My country—right or wrong." Obviously, such a state of mind lent itself to easy manipulation by despots and nationalistic leaders who were able to send millions of young people to die on the battlefield in the name of patriotic duty. As such, nationalism became a new cause for warfare, inflicting unspeakable misery on millions of people throughout the centuries.

While nationalistic sentiments still continue to operate within the destructive plane, the constructive process has already given rise to a new stage of expansion in the primary unit of human identity toward "world citizenship." The embryo of this new consciousness was first conceived on May 23, 1844, following the transmission of the first telegraph, an event that removed the age-old barriers of time and space from the life of humanity and, as such, began to pose inherent contradictions and challenges to the nationalistic mindset. The challenge to the nationalistic mindset has since grown exponentially in magnitude and scope, with the rapidly multiplying technological advances in transportation and communication that have enabled people around the globe to communicate and interact with each other instantaneously. International trade, economic interdependence, migration, interracial marriage and the mobility of people of various backgrounds who have fanned out throughout the planet; all of these factors have increasingly moved our world closer to becoming a global melting pot. The exploration of outer space and the ability to see and conceptualize our planet as one homeland for all of humanity, furthermore, has stretched and enlarged the exclusive nationalistic boundaries with which people used to identify in the past.

In addition, it is increasingly clear that, in the twenty-first century, humanity faces challenges that cannot be resolved by any one country, including security and climate change. We have already arrived at a point in human history where we would not be able to function in any area of life, not even to get on a plane for overseas travel, without regional and international collaborative exchanges and agreements. The new globally connected generation, in particular, is increasingly comfortable with the idea of world citizenship, and the trend is measurably on the upswing among the millennials in the United States.

This movement toward growing global interdependence has presented a serious challenge to the nationalistic mindset in various parts of the world. Beyond creating discomfort among populations who continue to cling to exclusive identities that give them a sense of pride, the intermingling of races due to migration across the continents has given rise to intercultural tensions. As globalization transforms the familiar contours of national economies and requires people to gain new skills and attain higher educational levels in order to remain competitive, furthermore, those with previously well-paying jobs, such as the older blue-collar workers in western countries, blame trade agreements and immigrants for their plight. The fact that many blue-collar workers are not willing to engage in the type of hard menial labor that immigrants provide, or that many national industries (e.g., the agricultural sector in the United States) rely on immigrants for their survival, appears to make little difference in these strongly held beliefs. The subsequent surge in angry sentiments among these populations provides politicians in search of divide-and-conquer scenarios with a ready pool of highly motivated constituents. With a nationalistic mindset ripe to eagerly consume "populist" propaganda, these blue-collar workers support nationalistic leaders who fan the flames of xenophobia and argue in favor of putting "our nation first," closing national borders and restricting international trade; all of which, they are told, would help bring back jobs and restore their economic prosperity.

Clearly, the accelerating trend toward growing interdependence among nations cannot be reversed. At the same time, we must acknowledge that certain economic aspects of globalization, driven by the greed of multinational corporations who tend to follow the path of least resistance to exploiting unregulated cheap labor, have exacerbated the inequitable economic conditions, both within and among nations. Despite overall GDP growth in many countries, the gains among different economic classes have been uneven and, in many cases, have resulted in growing gaps between the haves and have-nots. As such, the unchecked ability of powerful multinational corporations to exploit cheap labor across the globe has been a key enabler of many politicians in recent years to execute divide-and-conquer tactics within the destructive plane. As a result we are, once again, witness to the stirrings of tumultuous nationalism by power-mongers who have historically succeeded in manipulating uninformed groups.

The Brexit vote, which led Britain out of the European Union by a 52 percent to 48 percent margin, won precisely because of the ability of such politicians to engage in nostalgic propaganda. This time, the constructive voices of the younger generation, the vast majority of whom voted in favor of enlarged loyalties and regional cooperation, fell short of the needed majority. The vote has already had negative economic consequences. Shortly after the announcement of the outcome of the Brexit vote, the British pound sterling fell precipitously, stocks lost major ground and there was a freeze in investments in the United Kingdom. In a rare case of agreement among economists, Brexit is expected to do little to boost the country's economic and political standing in the world; instead, the vote is expected to isolate the country politically and hurt the British economy substantially in the coming years.

By all accounts, it may not be long before the misdirected anger reflected in the Brexit vote will wreak such economic havoc as to accelerate the collapse of the tottering nationalistic institutions and mindsets in Britain and make it clear, once and for all, that trying to turn back the clock to return to a world organized on the basis of nationalistic supremacy is a futile endeavor.

Although "globalization" has many different definitions and means different things to different people, the accelerating movement toward increasing awareness, exchange and interdependence among the people of various cultures is a reality that will continue to move forward in the twenty-first century. It is clear, however, that we must work to ensure that the benefits of globalization accrue equitably within and among nations.

## Religious Strife

Throughout history, strife among followers of different religions, as well as the people who believe in various interpretations of the teachings of the same Prophet, was a major cause of war. Despite making positive contributions to the advancement of human civilization, religions did not remain immune, either to a natural aging process or to the corrupting influence of the human quest for supremacy and power.

Soon after its founding, every religion was subjected to gradual change, often on the basis of self-serving interpretations of its original teachings by some of its more sophisticated followers. As each of these followers emerged as a religious leader in his own right and gained a following on the basis of his particular interpretations of religious doctrine, the religion was divided into an increasing number of sects, each focusing on a particular aspect of the Prophet's original teachings. Ultimately, the desire within each splinter group to assert its righteousness and supremacy over all others led to an outbreak of religious conflict, often culminating in bloody warfare. Such sectarian conflicts, of course, only added to the religious conflicts dividing the followers of different Prophets. Ultimately, through a bewildering process of division, contamination and perversion, the original purpose of religion (i.e., love) was turned into its direct opposite (i.e., hate).

As such, the teachings of every major Founder of Faith may be likened to a fresh and pure spring bubbling up on top of a high mountain, which in its original state was capable of reviving anyone dying of thirst. As it has come down the mountain, however, it has been increasingly polluted by man-made toxins. Not surprisingly, by the time it has reached the sea, it can kill anyone who drinks from it.

As they have become divided and polluted, and their light has been obscured by superstition, fanaticism and dogma, religions have proven to be a useful context for power-mongers in which to satisfy their thirst for power. Like racism and nationalism, religious fanaticism has lent itself well to the purposes of demagogues who would use any means to whip the masses into a frenzy of unquestionable loyalty to their own self-aggrandizing ends.

Yet, among all of the destructive factors that have brought division, injustice and death to human society, religious strife has been perhaps the most tragic. Because, if we study the original teachings of the major world religions, we will find that the purpose of religion throughout history has been to awaken human beings to their spiritual nature, to inculcate moral and ethical values and to promote harmony and peace. Close examination of the original teachings of the world's major religions—including those of Judaism, Hinduism, Buddhism, Zoroastrianism, Christianity, Islam and the Baha'i Faith—will reveal a clear commonality in their spiritual teachings. The universal ethical principle, "do unto others as you will have them do unto you," is a basic teaching repeated in almost exactly the same words in the scriptures of all religions, and the admonishments against killing, stealing and lying are also shared by all religions.

This fact becomes demonstrably clear if we take the time to review a few brief quotes from the original authoritative scriptures of these religions.

*"Love your neighbor as yourself."*

*"May love triumph over contempt."*

*"That one I love who is incapable of ill will, who is friendly and compassionate."*

*"As a mother with her own life guards the life of her own child, let all-embracing thoughts for all that lives be thine."*

*"Love your enemies, do good to those who hate you, bless those who curse you, pray for those who abuse you."*

*"What actions are most excellent? To gladden the heart of a human being, to feed the hungry, to help the afflicted, to lighten the sorrows of the sorrowful, and to remove the wrongs of the injured."*

*"Ye are the fruits of one tree, and the leaves of one branch. Deal ye one with another with the utmost love and harmony, with friendliness and fellowship."*

*"Have we not all one father? Has not one God created us? Why then are we faithless to one another, profaning the covenant of our fathers?"*

*"Listen to all that you hear and do not repeat it at random. Do not mock at anyone."*

*"Strive constantly to serve the welfare of the world... Do your work with the welfare of others always in mind."*

*"Think not of the faults of others, of what they have done or not done. Think rather of your own sins, of the things you have done or not done."*

*"Put on then... compassion, kindness, lowliness, meekness, and patience, forbearing one another and, if one has a complaint against another, forgiving each other; as the Lord has forgiven you."*

*"Let there be no compulsion in religion."*

*"Consort with the followers of all religions in a spirit of friendliness and fellowship."*

*"You shall not be partial in judgment; you shall hear the small and the great alike; you shall not be afraid of the face of man, for the judgment is God's."*

*"Do not do unto others what would not be good for yourselves."*

*"One should not behave towards others in a way which is disagreeable to oneself. This is the essence of morality."*

*"He who for the sake of happiness does not hurt others, who also want happiness, shall hereafter find happiness."*

*"God shows no partiality, but in every nation anyone who fears him and does what is right is acceptable to him."*

*"Stand out firmly for justice, as witnesses to God even as against yourselves or your parents, or your kin, and whether it be (against) rich or poor."*

*"If thine eyes be turned towards justice, choose thou for thy neighbor that which thou choose for thyself."*

*"They shall beat their swords into plowshares, and their spears into pruning hooks; nation shall not lift up sword against nation, neither shall they study war anymore."*

*"May peace triumph over discord."*

*"They live in wisdom who see themselves in all and all in themselves."*

*"Better than a thousand useless words is one single word that gives peace."*

*"Put your sword back into its place; for all who take the sword will perish by the sword."*

*"The same religion has He established for you as that which He enjoined on Noah, Abraham, Moses and Jesus; namely, that ye should remain steadfast in Religion, and make no divisions therein."*

*"It is incumbent upon all peoples of the world to reconcile their differences, and, with perfect unity and peace, abide beneath the shadow of the Tree of His care and loving-kindness."*

(Key: Quotes are from the original scriptures of Judaism, Hinduism, Buddhism, Zoroastrianism, Christianity, Islam and the Baha'i Faith, in that order, on the topics of love, justice, respect and peace. Source: Harold Rosen (2010), *Founders of Faith*.)

In addition to the commonality in their moral teachings, all religions offer very similar concepts of the ultimate purpose and meaning of life and share a fundamental belief in the existence of a human soul, a Higher Being and an afterlife. And, regardless of how these concepts are expressed, the thrust of the teachings remains on the need for purification of the soul, movement toward the Higher Being and the attainment of salvation and everlasting life.

While religions share the same basic spiritual principles, they do differ in their social teachings as well as in the way they have presented and explained their ethical principles, reflecting their response to the intellectual capacity and social needs of human beings at different stages of their development.

As previously mentioned, a basic recognition of the essential commonalities among religions began to emerge in the late nineteenth century as a key component of the constructive collective consciousness and was reflected in the first ever Parliament of World Religions held in Chicago in 1893. The chairman of the parliament, John Henry Barrows, described the purpose of the gathering as follows: "The solemn charge which the Parliament preaches to all true believers is a return to the primitive unity of the world... The results may be far off, but they are certain." That desire for unity among religions, expressed formally by the religious leaders represented at that historic gathering, has since grown into a robust global interfaith movement. During the parliament's centennial celebration in Chicago in 1993, the participating religious leaders collectively declared and embraced a common "global ethic" and, after a number of other gatherings, resolved to take collaborative action on critical issues facing humanity during the parliament's 2015 meeting in Salt Lake City.

In the United States, a growing interfaith consciousness is reflected in the shrinking of the long-standing religious and social rifts between Catholics and Protestants and a palpable search to move beyond denominational lines in the context of ecumenical and Unitarian movements. The most important evidence of the operation of the constructive collective consciousness in the United States, however, is that religious intolerance and bigotry, while still alive and well in the hearts of many, has been put on the defensive and has lost its former legitimacy. While it is still possible for a preacher to condemn people of other religions to the fire of hell in a church sermon, he/she can expect swift repudiation for expressing such views in public. And, despite the strident efforts of the old guards of religious intolerance, increasingly fewer people in the United States are willing to indict all people of a particular religion for the extremism displayed by a small minority.

At the international level, religious persecution and denial of guaranteed human rights based on religion have been strongly condemned by the United Nations and international law, and a wide range of organizations work to combat the spread of hate and persecution based on religious belief.

On a completely different front, another kind of challenge is being presented to religious fundamentalism and prejudice by many people of intelligence and goodwill who, disillusioned by the grand follies of history in the name of religion, are either abandoning religion altogether or increasingly identifying themselves as "spiritual, but not religious," seeking guidance in various meditative practices and traditions. These are the people who have recognized the toxicity of the water but are still searching to find the original, pure spring. In so far as they consider the lack of religion better than having a religion that divides humanity and are searching for a path to a unifying consciousness, they represent an important dynamic element within the constructive process.

## Gender Inequality

In the common discourse, inequality of women and men is less often associated with being a root cause of war. Yet, gender inequality has been an even more insidious incubator of violence and war in human society than racism, nationalism and religious strife.

To illustrate the connection between gender inequality and violence, it is important to go back several millennia in history and ask a simple question: Why did the male of the species become socially and politically dominant to begin with?

The primary starting point for the historical differentiation between men and women was the fact that women were the only one of the two sexes who could bear children. This biological fact initially created a solely practical division of labor between men and women, with women staying at home and nurturing their children and men going out to hunt for food and taking responsibility for defending the territory occupied by women and children. Although both women and men made equally vital contributions to the social organization, as time went on this division of labor gradually led to a system of advantage and privilege for men; their labor came to be deemed more valuable, and the vital work that women did was progressively devalued. The resulting social organization, in which the male became dominant over the female, was then reinforced by other factors, including the male's relatively greater physical strength.

This imbalance in the value given to the masculine versus the feminine legitimized and glorified being a "warrior" (associated with being strong) over being a "peacemaker" (associated with being weak). It gave superior rights and privileges to the masculine over the feminine and became the primary incubator for supremacy-seeking and aggression. As such, one might propose that the course of human history went terribly wrong when a simple division of labor, which began as a result of practical considerations, devolved into a lopsided social system that initially bred, then glorified and ultimately perpetuated forceful violence.

The systemic power acquired by the male-dominated consciousness appropriated the semantic realm and shaped all reality in human societies across the globe.

Throughout the ages, not only cultural beliefs, but also all forms of social scientific discoveries, including Darwin's theories of evolution, were interpreted in this context. The result was the reification of an erroneous and, indeed, dangerous truism that "all human beings are aggressive by nature." Like many other predominant truisms in the world, the belief in the incorrigibly aggressive nature of people was a product of a male-dominated society in which the term "human being" was equated with the male of the species. In its obvious sexism, this expression lost sight of the fact that women, comprising half of the world's population, were predominantly non-aggressive. Thus, inequality of women and men became a root cause of war in three major ways. First, it glorified masculine warrior values. Second, it kept humanity from even attempting to work toward a peaceful world by paralyzing the collective will and deceiving us into believing that eliminating aggression is a hopeless endeavor. And, third, it suppressed the woman's voice and point of view, whose equal participation in international decision-making would otherwise have helped bring about an emphasis on peaceful resolution rather than aggressive and bloody settlement of international conflicts.

During the last few decades, the constructive collective consciousness has opened an important new frontier in scientific inquiry about human nature. The emerging science has increasingly pointed to the fact that the male's predominant tendency toward aggression is not a result of an inherent biological mechanism. Rather, it is largely the result of such environmental factors as the centuries-long domination of men over women, which has led to the creation of a male culture based primarily on the glorification of aggression as a proof of "manhood." From early childhood, most boys are taught to be "tough" and ready to use force as a means of getting their way in disputes. These attitudes, along with the false and harmful stereotypes of what it means to be a man or a woman, are then perpetuated in the school and the work place and reinforced by the mass media. It is this constant conditioning of men to seek glory in being a warrior that is, in large part, responsible for the continuing tendency on the part of men to be more aggressive than women.

Contemporary scientific studies of human evolution, furthermore, support the understanding that the capacity for compassion, cooperation and even altruism, have been key ingredients in enabling the survival of human beings throughout the millennia and can become the primary modes in human relationships, if given the opportunity to flourish.

The emerging constructive consciousness in support of equal rights for women also has matured considerably since the nineteenth century. Although it took over seventy years after the passing of the "Declaration of Sentiments" at the Seneca Falls conference in 1848 for women to get the right to vote, the women's movement in the United States saw rapid acceleration in the 1970s and led to increasing awareness about the need to give equal value to feminine qualities. This emerging awareness was based on the realization that, although learning how to use sheer physical force to fight an enemy or to subdue an animal in the process of hunting for food was a useful skill centuries ago, physical force is no longer either necessary or useful for human survival. Most important today are intellectual power and the capability to develop and implement a blueprint for a peaceful and prosperous global society. In this process, it is intuition, a peaceful orientation and the ability to communicate, negotiate and cooperate that are most important. Given the superior skills of women in these areas, their equal participation in international decision-making is a major prerequisite for the achievement of a peaceful society. Once women are given equal opportunity to climb the social, corporate and political ranks—without being forced to abandon their feminine qualities in the process— their equal participation in world affairs is bound to temper the aggressive male culture, enabling men to seek the proof of their manhood no longer in their ability to win a fight, but in a noble character conducive to the achievement of a compassionate and peaceful world.

Another important factor in this growing consciousness has been the extensive research conducted in the field of international development. Development agencies, such as the UNDP and related NGOs, have discovered, through many years of research and practice, that the most important single factor for success in sustainable development is education and empowerment of women. A vast body of research on this topic has clearly shown that increasing gender equality improves GDP, health and other measures of development and prosperity in every community. When women are empowered, their families, communities and countries prosper. On the other hand, when outworn gender roles are strictly enforced, the men, as well as the women, suffer negative consequences.

The global dimension of the negative effects of male gender roles on men and their families was brought into focus in two books published by Oxford University Press in 2000, entitled *Voices of the Poor: Crying for Change*, and *Can Anyone Hear Us?* The research detailed in these books was conducted by the International Monetary Fund (IMF) in an effort to identify the causes of poverty by listening to the voices of the poor themselves and featured the results of extensive interviews with men and women in twenty developing countries, covering a large geographic area, ranging from Gabon and Swaziland, to Ecuador and Latvia, to India and Vietnam. The most significant and unexpected finding of this body of research was the destructive effect of masculine gender roles on men's ability to adapt to changing economic circumstances and how this phenomenon exacerbated poverty.

Among other things, these studies showed that, as men were laid off from their traditional jobs and lost their ability to be the primary breadwinners, they experienced disorienting challenges to their perceptions of themselves as "providers and heads of families." This would, subsequently, lead to a deep sense of emasculation, frustration and anger, which was invariably expressed in the form of domestic violence, alcoholism, depression, abandonment of wife and children, isolation and even suicide.

In the face of the loss of their traditional jobs, these men found themselves unable to take a job of lower status because of masculine pride. Under these circumstances, the women would go out and do any type of work they could possibly find in the informal sector, including extremely low-income, low-status and high risk jobs, in order to feed their families. A major tragedy for the families in which the men were unable to adapt to this role-reversal, however, was that the hard-earned income of the women would be confiscated by force and spent on alcohol, gambling and other means of escaping reality. Ultimately, the strict male gender roles were found to cause these men to lose the opportunity to adapt and build a better life for their families. Instead, they fell into self-destructive patterns of behavior, resulting in great loss for themselves, their families and their communities. The small percentage of the men who were able to accept the new arrangements and collaborate with their spouses, however, succeeded in helping their families to thrive despite economic hardship.

The negative effects of strict male gender roles have also been the subject of recent focus in social-scientific research in the United States. In his 1998 book entitled *Real Boys: Rescuing Our Sons from the Myths of Boyhood*, Harvard psychologist William Pollack made an important scholarly contribution to starting a conversation about how strict gender roles undermine the well-being of adolescent boys. Bringing together his findings from interviews and clinical work with more than 150 teenage boys, Pollack provided evidence of how these masculine gender roles, or what he calls the "Boy Code," have been operating in destructive ways in the lives of boys in the United States.

One of Pollack's major insights is that, similar to all other human beings, boys experience the full range of human emotions, including love, fear, shame, guilt, sadness, vulnerability, uncertainty and low self-esteem. Among all of these and other natural feelings, the only emotion boys have full social license to express is anger. This lack of support in family and society for emotional expression forces boys to avoid expressing their fears and disappointments from a young age and to keep their feelings bottled up only to release them through violent bursts of anger and aggression.

This process of "gender straight-jacketing" has resulted in serious harm to boys and men, as well as to the American society as a whole. During the last three decades, in particular, boys have progressively fallen behind girls academically and have had a higher incidence of serious mental illness. They have also become increasingly more prone to committing suicide, at a rate four times higher than that among girls.

When it comes to the mass shootings that have happened in the United States during the last decade, we find that almost all of them were committed by young men, the vast majority of whom were white males. The expectation of privilege (i.e., being entitled to a girl, a job and a successful future) is an added source of rage for many young men, which combined with the gendered expectation to keep their fear and sadness to themselves, exacerbates their tendency to develop serious mental illness leading to devastating harm to themselves and others.

This epidemic of young males committing mass murder is certainly not a phenomenon limited to the United States. The "Boy Code" is very much a universal one, and the havoc it continues to wreak in societies around the world in various forms is an intimate feature of the destructive plane.

With the educational and professional opportunities available to women in the United States, on the other hand, the younger generation of American women has succeeded in breaking almost all of the barriers that stood in the path of realizing their full potential. Today, American women have not only closed many of the previous gaps, they have achieved excellence in every field previously reserved for the male of the species.

The visible level of progress by women has created a strong challenge for the destructive mindset in the United States and has led to resistance by those men who believe, self-destructively, that their interests are being threatened and must be preserved. In the United States, the defensive measures of the warriors of the old order have taken the form of vilification of the cause of women's equality and an anti-feminist ideology reflected in the use of such words as "feminazi" and the promotion of nostalgia for returning to the days when machismo was unapologetically glorified.

A conspicuous response by the destructive process in various other parts of the world in which women have been gaining access to education and entering previously male-dominated professional and political arenas has been that shown by extremist religious groups, such as those that spearheaded the Islamic Revolution in Iran and the Taliban in Afghanistan and Pakistan. Finding the threat to their patriarchal societies intolerable, both regimes instituted harsh rules to reverse the emancipation of women in their countries, including removing them from their professional positions and forcing them to wear veils and burkas. The extremism of the Taliban, in particular, was clearly reflected in their response to a fourteen-year-old girl, Malala Yousafzai, whom they shot in the head simply because she had the courage to stand up for girls' rights to an education.

The fact that Malala survived that attack, and went on to be awarded the Nobel Peace Prize and become a celebrated global voice in defense of women's education, is a clear testament to the forward march of the constructive process despite the bloody attempts of those who linger in the tottering structures of the destructive plane.

Indeed, all of the reactionary efforts to try to stem the forward march of history toward gender equality have only served to further energize the constructive mindset. An important sign of this growing consciousness is the fact that, in addition to the gendered division of labor, the second and more insidious prong of gender inequality, namely, sexual objectification of women, has been recognized as the destructive phenomenon that it is. It has become increasingly clear that, despite the near elimination of the division of labor between women and men in many countries, the male fantasy of sexual domination of women (i.e., being forever out on the "hunt" to "conquer" women sexually) remains alive and well within the destructive plane.

This persistent male fantasy takes on a variety of forms in different cultural contexts. In Western countries, it is perpetuated in portrayals of women in much of the visual advertising that upholds unrealistic standards of feminine beauty and continues to socialize young girls with the idea that their primary goal in life should be to become an object of pursuit and desire for men by striving for a perfect body (a large bust and a small waist) showcased in revealing clothing. It is also reflected in the sexual violence that continues to be perpetrated by young men against young women, even in such centers of high culture and education as college campuses, with the women being assumed guilty until proven innocent.

The challenge to sexual objectification of women has been a more recent phenomenon created by the constructive process. Even so, it has gained enough momentum in the twenty-first century to delegitimize the dominant male discourse on sexual harassment. What was long dismissed as "locker room banter," is no longer an acceptable form of machismo; it has now acquired the status of an indefensible and shameful behavior.

The collective consciousness about the importance of addressing sexual objectification of women is also gaining strength in other, more traditional societies. Increasingly, more women are raising their voices against the harsh measures that not only keep them inside the home and deprive them of education, but, in many societies, also cover them up physically to prevent them from tempting the "natural" lustful desire of men to hunt and conquer them. A notable example of such protests is the online movement, "My Stealthy Freedom," in Iran, founded by Masih Alinejad, a journalist of Iranian origin based in London. Through widely shared Facebook posts, Iranian women, who have been forced to wear the hijab against their will, have been posting pictures of themselves with their hair flowing in the wind. A large number of Iranian men have also joined this movement by wearing a hijab in the pictures as a sign of protest against the compulsory dress code imposed on women in Iran.

It is extremely important to point out that, whenever wearing a head-cover reflects a conscious choice made by a woman herself, that choice must be respected and upheld. Whether a woman chooses to wear a hijab or a bikini, that choice, in and of itself, would hardly be a sign of male-domination. However, in general, both the covered female body in traditional societies and the exposed female body in western countries are dictated by rules and preferences imposed on girls through socialization in male-dominated cultures. For that reason, current dress codes for women across the globe may be considered to have evolved as glaring emblems of gender inequality. Both dress codes may, in fact, be considered as two sides of the same coin, molded by internalized patriarchy.

Despite the ongoing oppression of women in too many parts of the world, the movement toward gender equality has grown steadily across the globe during the last two centuries. Much like racism, sexism has been delegitimized, and those who try to defend it will continue to face increasing social condemnation. Once a harmful mindset has been delegitimized, no amount of strident effort will succeed in normalizing it. Today, the constructive collective consciousness is increasingly clear about the fact that gender equality is not just a women's issue; it is a human issue. And its achievement is a fundamental prerequisite for peace.

## Extremes of Wealth and Poverty

Throughout much of human history, blatant domination and exploitation was the primary blueprint in economic life. As recently as the nineteenth century, feudal lords exploited their peasants, plantation owners exploited their slaves, capitalists exploited their workers and imperialist powers exploited their colonized lands and populations. The Industrial Revolution, which had fueled the process of colonial domination of resource-rich lands by the western imperialist powers, exacerbated these processes of domination and exploitation throughout the nineteenth century. It also gave rise to the technological and economic advantages that ultimately drew the lines of demarcation between the so-called "advanced industrial" and "less developed" countries.

Full-fledged capitalism remained dominant throughout the nineteenth century, and the multiplying advantages gained by the capitalists who held not only the capital, but also the means of production, continued to exacerbate the vast economic gaps within and among nations. In contrast to the vision depicted in the eighteenth century writings of Adam Smith, who had upheld the pursuit of self-interest in a free market as a fundamentally moral act, the prevailing brute capitalism served the interests of the wealthy elites and subjugated the economic well-being of the vast majority of people around the globe.

A harsh critique was leveled against brute capitalism in the nineteenth century by Karl Marx who berated it for its unbridled greed and unabashed exploitation of labor and advocated revolutionary action by the members of the working class to transform the prevailing pattern in economic relationships. The Marxist alternative sought to equalize the distribution of wealth in society by eliminating the capitalist competition for profit and replacing it with a centrally planned cooperative economy. Having removed profit as the primary motivator for hard work, it sought to generate productivity by indoctrinating workers into a sense of solidarity based on economic class.

The Marxist ideology inspired major revolutions in two of the largest nations in the world, among others, during the twentieth century, one by Lenin in Russia (1917) and the other by Mao in China (1949), both of which failed to achieve the communist utopia. In a sense, the practical application of Marxism, originally aimed at putting the power in the hands of the people in a truly "democratic" and egalitarian system, became perverted much like a religion, creating devastating excesses in what ultimately became exceedingly totalitarian regimes.

Among many other factors, the failure of communism was due to an inherent paradox. Despite its genesis as a fiercely materialistic ideology that denied and suppressed transcendent spiritual impulses, it expected people to set aside their self-interest to serve the collective interests of the proletariat. Although the communist doctrine was internalized by a minority, it remained a coercive ritual for the majority of people in communist countries. Driven primarily by force and fear, rather than voluntary initiative rooted in a personal moral choice, communism failed to present a viable alternative to capitalism.

Despite its failure in practice, the Marxist critique inspired a flourishing consciousness about the "excesses of capitalism." It sparked a process of maturation in the collective consciousness, leading to a number of major economic innovations in the twentieth century to moderate the economic inequities inherent in the pursuit of unbridled capitalism. These innovations included the development of workers' unions and welfare systems and the implementation of "socialist" ideals in various European and Scandinavian countries.

It became increasingly clear to the collective consciousness throughout the twentieth century that people do not begin their journey through life from the same starting point, and they seldom have equal opportunities or operate under similar conditions. From the moment they are born, the children of the poor begin their life at a disadvantage. As poor children they are likely to have lesser access to adequate nourishment, a healthy environment, quality education and the many other essential ingredients of socioeconomic success. Though a few may succeed in breaking out of the cycle of poverty, most are likely to become menial workers like their parents, toiling for minimum wage to produce higher and higher profits for their wealthy employers. This inherent tendency in the capitalist competition to cumulatively disadvantage the poor workers while rewarding the capitalist owners, was recognized as a primary mechanism responsible for persistent and widening economic gaps between the rich and the poor.

The constructive consciousness about the far-reaching social impact of brute capitalism gained visible momentum in 1994 at a gathering of business leaders from the United States, Japan and several European countries at Caux, a small hamlet in Switzerland, who had come together to develop a set of new principles for "moral capitalist decision-making." The innovative product of that historic gathering was the Caux Roundtable Principles for Business, which, for the first time in history, formalized a code of ethics for moral capitalism. As Stephen Young, the Global Executive Director of the Roundtable, has explained in his book, *Moral Capitalism* (2003), the Roundtable participants concluded that successful businesses need far more than financial capital to be able to sustain their financial growth long-term; they also need social capital, reputational capital, physical capital and human capital.

Following that historic gathering, many empirical studies have been conducted on the relationship between ethical business behavior and sustainable company profitability. The results have confirmed that businesses that remain cognizant of their responsibility to their workers and to society (stakeholders) tend to be substantially more profitable and sustainable than businesses that focus on short-term financial gain for their shareholders. In other words, these studies have shown that moral capitalism is not only good for the workers, the society and the environment; it is also good for capitalists. Historical evidence, including that produced by the large number of business failures at the turn of the twenty-first century in the United States (e.g., Enron, Tyco, WorldCom, JP Morgan Chase and many others), which were found to be rooted in corrupt leadership and business practices, have made it abundantly clear that upholding ethical principles in business decision-making is not just a moral responsibility; it is a strategic necessity.

The growing constructive consciousness in the business arena has been responsible for many innovative and unprecedented practices that have gained visibility and momentum in the twenty-first century. New business leadership models such as "leadership as service," innovative employee-centered approaches, such as work-life balance, flextime, parental leave, college tuition remission, profit-sharing and the many other emerging socially-responsible business models that care about humanitarian issues, fair trade and environmental sustainability, are all different manifestations of this growing constructive consciousness.

Among all of these innovative approaches, profit-sharing presents perhaps the most effective and systemic means of addressing the extremes of wealth and poverty within and among nations. A key feature of the profit-sharing concept is a promising synthesis of the important concepts of "incentive" in capitalism and "equity" in communism. In a profit-sharing system both the capitalists and the workers share in the company profits. As such, profit-sharing maximizes the workers' incentive to do their best in the workplace by giving them a stake in the profits. At the same time, it removes the excesses of capitalistic exploitation and helps achieve an equitable distribution of wealth. Ultimately, profit-sharing is likely to increase not only the wages of the workers, but also the net profit gained by the owners because of the higher worker productivity.

The consciousness about the need to increase the workers' stakes in a company's success has spread visibly throughout the business world during the past decade, and a number of companies have adopted various iterations of this paradigm. Despite its great promise to yield a win-win outcome for both capitalists and workers, however, the rate of adoption for profit-sharing systems has been slower than expected. This is perhaps because taking the first step toward profit-sharing requires a deliberate moral commitment on the part of the company owners. It requires that capitalists abandon their exploitation of their workers for immediate gain and show a true caring for their workers before they themselves reap its benefits. It entails a voluntary sharing of wealth, though it promises to benefit the rich as well as the poor. As an approach based on moral as well as economic concepts, profit-sharing exemplifies the importance of voluntary adoption of moral principles in resolving national and global economic problems.

Clearly, for this and other models of moral capitalism to be more widely adopted, the mindset depicting business as a zero-sum game of winners and losers needs to be transformed. The collective consciousness in the realm of business and commerce must fully evolve to recognize that sustainable corporate success in the twenty-first century requires the adoption of win-win approaches and a voluntary application of moral principles. This will not only lead to greater financial gains for capitalists, but it will also serve to mitigate the large economic gaps between rich and poor, both within and among nations.

The urgency of addressing the vast economic disparities among nations was recognized by the United Nations early in its founding as an integral part of its efforts toward achieving a more peaceful world. At a time when the rapid process of decolonialization had produced a large number of countries struggling for true political independence and economic development, the decade of the 1960s was designated by the United Nations as the UN Development Decade. More than three decades of international activity by the United Nations and its related organizations and NGOs, however, produced little sustainable development. The small improvements, when they did occur, primarily benefited the rich rather than the poor, and the overall gaps between the advanced and developing countries increased. Well into the 1990s, a stark contrast between deprivation and overconsumption was still visible throughout the world, reflected in the images of children with distended bellies starving in Africa, juxtaposed with the luxurious vagaries of large numbers of people in developed countries, for whom the primary daily struggle consisted of how to stay "slim and trim" in an environment of abundance and over-indulgence.

Throughout the latter part of the twentieth century, the frustration of the masses and leaders in the Third World countries with the slow pace of their own development as they watched their former colonizers achieve new technological and economic frontiers, kept the fire of suspicion and bitterness burning and created an explosive potential for conflict and war. Even in those areas of the globe that had been lifted out of extreme poverty, people continued to be reminded of their relative deprivation, whether at the sight of the gated communities designed to keep them out, or the media images of the good life in the richer countries. These lingering extremes in wealth and poverty also cultivated an inferiority complex that often reinforced the tendency on the part of the political leaders in these countries to seek fulfillment and glory not in the painstaking, gradual and often uncertain process of national development, but in the "quick fix" of regional military superiority.

One of the most dangerous current examples of this tendency is the ongoing saga in North Korea—a country whose young leader, Kim Jong Un, continues to seek international recognition by starving his people in pursuit of nuclear military power. This tragedy continues after a missed opportunity in 2012 when, in a complex scenario, the United States decided to turn down the new leader's request for food and economic aid in exchange for dismantling the country's uranium enrichment program.

As these leaders squander their nation's meager resources on stockpiles of armaments, they serve to exacerbate the fragile economic conditions and widen the characteristically large gaps between the wealthy elites and poor masses. These internal economic gaps, in turn, create their own potential for instability. Leaders who ignore the economic disparities between the "haves" and "have-nots" in their countries risk being toppled by the seemingly powerless but angry masses ready to rush to the help of revolutionary leaders. The recurrent coups and revolutions in Third World countries—often bloody events which get rid of one dictator only to replace him with another, while doing little to improve the lot of the masses—are clearly indicative of the destabilizing effects of poverty within nations.

From a western perspective, many of the revolutions in various parts of the world have tended to be interpreted as reflections of "people power" movements in search of democratic alternatives. Yet, closer examination of these movements, including the Islamic Revolution in Iran (1979), the Tiananmen uprising in China (1989) and even the Arab Spring uprising in Egypt (2011), shows that, despite their unique complexities, they all had one important element in common: anger and frustration on the part of young people, rooted in relative economic deprivation. The watchword that fueled the zeal of the masses for Khomeini's rise to power in Iran, beyond his religious status, was his feigned concern for the "mostz'afin" (the poor). The university students who led the protests in China were searching for better economic prospects than the meager salaries they could expect after completing their higher education, and the common cause that bound the young people together at Tahrir Square in Egypt was their desire for economic opportunities unavailable to them under Mubarak.

The field of international development suffered through many failures throughout the twentieth century as it grappled with the difficult task of effecting sustainable economic development. The silver lining in these growing pains, however, was the fact that, by the end of the millennium, they had yielded many new lessons and best practices for more effective and sustainable development. Among these, two key realizations were the most important. First, international development fails when funds are allocated on the basis of political considerations and in exchange for explicit or implicit concessions, rather than on the basis of a true desire to help the developing nations. And, second, the grand plans for Third World development cannot be conceived and executed without regard for the true needs and wishes of the local population; neither can they be achieved in a top-down process by foreign experts who, far from respecting the local people's expertise or understanding their cultural values, view the local population as "backward" people in need of complete cultural transformation based on western models and values.

The work during the twenty-first century on achieving the Millennium Development Goals (MDG) benefited greatly from these lessons. The 2015 UN report on the status of the MDG announced that, among other advances, the goal of cutting "extreme poverty" (living below $1.90 per day) by 50 percent had been achieved ahead of schedule by 2010.

Although definitions of "poverty" and "extreme poverty" remain fluid as the World Bank grapples with precisely pinpointing the concept, reports indicate that, as of 1990, 40 percent of the people in the world lived in poverty. By 2015 that figure had been reduced to 10 percent. In addition, according to the International Monetary Fund forecasts, the developing economies of the world can expect a solid 4.2 percent growth rate in the years leading up to 2020. This includes many countries on the African continent that are making rapid economic progress thanks to the availability of smartphone technology, which in recent years has allowed them to leapfrog beyond their longstanding struggle to achieve industrialization. The most significant economic gains in the developing world, however, have been made by China, which alone lifted eight hundred million people out of poverty between 1980 and 2015. Obviously, the national and international development work needs to continue until the remaining three billion people in the world, who still live on less than $2.50 per day, are rescued from their plight.

No matter how successful the endeavors toward eradicating poverty, the extreme *disparity* in wealth between the rich and the poor across the globe remains a critically destabilizing force that must be addressed head-on, both within and among nations. It is, indeed, inconceivable that in the United States the wealth gap between the top 1 percent and the middle class stands at 1,000,000 percent. Equally staggering is the fact that the United States, with 4.5 percent of the world's population, controls 42 percent of the personal wealth in the world. Globally, the top 1 percent of wealthy individuals control 50 percent of the wealth.

Despite the many technical and economic complexities involved in alleviating such extremes in wealth and poverty, ultimately it is the extent of moral commitment on the part of the individuals involved that will determine the nature of the outcome. Only when the advanced nations of the world help the Third World countries on the basis of a true moral concern for the well-being of the people in these countries, rather than as a means of advancing their own foreign policy interests, will they be able to effect positive change. Only when the political leaders in the developing countries develop the moral discipline to refrain from siphoning off development aid money into their personal bank accounts will the funds find their way to those who most need it. Only when the foreign experts learn to abandon their racial and national prejudices and listen to and respect the culture of the people they seek to help, will they be able to develop appropriate plans and implement them in a way that attracts the support of the local community. And only when the local communities in the Third World are unified and organized at the grass-roots level and learn how to help develop their communities through consultation and collective effort, will sustainable and independent development become a reality in the Third World. Every one of these conditions, a true desire to help others, integrity and trustworthiness, a mind and heart open to other races and cultures, the ability to consult with and listen to others and the ability to unify and be unified, are all inherently moral in nature.

Clearly, the solution to the extremes of wealth and poverty within and among nations lies in the application not only of economic, but also of moral principles.

# Part 3: Terrorism—A Case Study

So far in this book we have identified racism, nationalism, religious strife, inequality of the sexes and extremes of wealth and poverty as the root causes of war. It would be appropriate, at this point, to examine the primary destructive trend of the twenty-first century (i.e., terrorism) as a case study to demonstrate how all of these root causes of war are reflected in this new form of violence and warfare. Although terrorism is closely identified in the collective consciousness with religious extremism, the fact is that all of the root causes of war discussed in this book fuel the phenomenon of terrorism and are used strategically by terrorist masterminds to propagate their cause.

Ironically, despite its development in the womb of the destructive order, terrorism poses an existential challenge to the most basic premise of that order—namely, the idea that a powerful centralized military force can be an effective means of defeating threats to national security.

Terrorism, as we know it today, is a relatively new phenomenon in human history. Acts of terror started as isolated events around the globe in the twentieth century and were carried out by a wide range of entities, including homegrown groups operating in the United States and Northern Ireland. However, they had, in large part, failed to attract the full attention of the world's leading centers of political and military power, until that fateful day in September 2001 when they literally struck the most prominent of these centers at the heart.

The shock and horror of such an unimaginably brazen act sent two of the most politically experienced and militarily powerful countries of the world, namely, the United States and the United Kingdom, into a frenzy of retaliatory decision-making conditioned by outworn approaches. Invade, bomb and kill the terrorists was the battle cry as thousands of soldiers were sent into Afghanistan and later into Iraq to wage a "War on Terror." Many years, trillions of dollars, and thousands of innocent lives later, what the world has to show for it is the accelerating spread of the cancer that is terrorism. Indeed, terrorism can be found at the heart of every war and crisis in the twenty-first century, from the fracturing of Iraq under ISIS, to the utter chaos and destruction in Syria, to the many other ongoing violent conflicts across the globe. Cyber-terrorism, a support system of this cancerous growth, comprises its most recent frontier.

With each military "victory" in pushing back ISIS from the territories it had captured in Iraq and Syria, there have been more attacks by organized cells and lone sympathizers on soft targets around the globe, including in Europe and the United States. The inability of military force to defeat terrorism or protect soft targets has reached a point where government officials and security experts simply look the public in the eye during media interviews and tell them there is nothing they can do to stop these attacks. They exclaim, matter-of-factly, that this is the "new normal," and that the best solution for each of us is to be vigilant and "say something when we see something." In the context of this bankruptcy of ideas, people continue to look to the false comfort offered by political leaders who promise to unleash even higher levels of military power to defeat terrorism.

In recent years, however, a new constructive consciousness has become increasingly palpable. A wide range of people, including scholars, security analysts and even political leaders, are asking deeper questions. Unlike a decade ago, when anyone trying to inquire about the causes of terrorism would have been accused of trying to "excuse" the terrorists' barbaric behavior, the constructive consciousness has made it increasingly more appropriate to ask a fundamental question: What are the factors that produce a ready pool of recruits for terrorism (i.e., young men who are willing to die in their twenties in suicide bombings that kill large numbers of innocent civilians)?

As a result of this new mode of inquiry, we now know much more than we did even a decade ago about the causes of "radicalization," a phenomenon that almost always precedes the act of joining a terrorist group. Evidence from an increasing number of studies, including a study based on leaked ISIS recruitment data, shows that the vast majority of those who join terrorist groups are young males who are poor and unemployed, or at best working in blue-collar jobs, with a very small percentage coming from white-collar professional backgrounds. Beyond poverty, these recruits, even when college-educated, have almost always experienced some form of alienation, discrimination and relative deprivation within their communities.

As Omer Taspinar, a prominent scholar on this topic has discussed in his 2009 article in *SAIS Review*, when we think about the background and motivations of those who join terrorist organizations, we must keep two important points in mind. First, there is a major distinction between the mastermind "elites" and their foot soldiers in terms of social and economic background within terrorist organizations. Bin Laden and Atta, the mastermind and the leader of the 9/11 attacks, respectively, had very different socio-economic backgrounds relative to the other Saudi men who participated in the attacks. This was so, even though the recruits who get selected for high-stakes terror operations are carefully screened for having the right level of education and skill to be successful. Unlike the image held by the average American, not every Saudi male comes from an affluent family; there are many pockets of poverty and a social hierarchy based on tribal background in Saudi Arabia. Second, we must make a distinction between "education" and "indoctrination" when measuring the educational level of those who participate in a terrorist act. Most terrorist foot soldiers have received their schooling, if any, as children in "madrasas" designed precisely for the purpose of radical indoctrination. In other cases, particularly among those brought up in western countries, terrorist propaganda often succeeds in appealing to the deep sense of alienation experienced by many intelligent young men.

Investigation by various other experts into the lives of the young men who have carried out terrorist attacks in Europe and the United States during the last decade, for example, has shown that the vast majority of them were driven by extreme rage, fueled by one or a combination of such factors as poverty, alienation, perceptions of real or imaginary injustice, male fantasy and last but not least, a search for purpose and meaning. All of the young people who join ISIS and carry out terrorist attacks may be considered to have one or more of these factors present in their radicalization process. Many of the known terrorist foot soldiers recruited in Europe were at some point alienated by an inability to fit in and perceived themselves as second-class citizens in their often segregated and impoverished neighborhoods.

Radicalization rooted in poverty and/or alienation, combined with fantasies of becoming a glorified "hero," comprises the common formula in making young men vulnerable to being recruited by terrorist masterminds not only in the western, but also in the developing countries. In Nigeria, for example, Boko Haram is successful in recruiting from the northern region of the country, where extreme poverty is rampant, and many other terrorist groups have also been successful in recruiting poverty-stricken young men from the slums of Casablanca in Morocco.

Thus, in order to address this cancerous growth in the body of humanity we must understand that, before an extremist "religious" cause succeeds in motivating bloody terrorist action, the foundation for joining it has already been built upon many other destructive factors.

Another important point is that the religious extremism expressed in acts of terror, far from representing a "clash of civilizations" between Islam and the West, serves as a tool to fan the flames of a smoldering violence already ignited by other root causes. More often than not, religious extremism is not the primary cause of terrorist action; it is the final motivator.

The disconnection between religious motivation and terrorism is also visible in the fact that terrorist acts kill far more Muslims and people of other religions in the Middle East than they kill Christians in the West. The worst terrorist attack during the bloody July of 2016, which coincided with the holy month of Ramadan, was carried out in Iraq and killed over two hundred people, more than the number killed in Orlando, Paris or Istanbul. Reports indicate that all of the victims in that attack were Muslim. Or consider the attack on July 4, 2016 by ISIS on the resting place of the Founder of Islam, Prophet Muhammad, in Medina, Saudi Arabia. This attack by Sunni terrorists in a Sunni country was denounced by many observers as an "attack on Islam itself" and should serve as clear evidence that religion, per se, often plays only a partial, if not nominal, role in terrorism.

Unlike the assumptions propagated by uninformed leaders, furthermore, it is not an entire religion that comprises the root cause of terrorism. In a vast number of cases, it is ethnic identities and sectarian enmities within the same religion that are directly visible in terrorism's signature. The sectarian strife between the Sunni minority (41 percent) and the Shia majority (52 percent) in Iraq has been a constant source of challenge to efforts by the United States to fight terrorism in the region. Consider that after the invasion of Iraq to wage a War on Terror in 2003, the United States spent an estimated 1.7-2.4 trillion dollars on the Iraq war itself (the total goes up to five trillion dollars when we include the war in Afghanistan), and another twenty-six billion dollars to train five hundred thousand Iraqi soldiers to defend their country. When a small band of one thousand ISIS members began to attack the US-trained Iraqi soldiers near Mosul (a city with a majority Sunni population) in 2014, over thirty thousand of the US-trained Iraqi soldiers surrendered without resistance, paving the way for an easy ISIS takeover. In this drama, sectarian and ethnic allegiance of the soldiers and inhabitants of the city to the Sunni background of ISIS, and their grievances against the Shia government in Baghdad, completely negated the vast military resources spent by the United States on erecting a barrier to terrorism in a country comprised of competing Sunni and Shia populations.

Another important fact to consider is that, in the military war against ISIS, it is primarily Muslim fighters who serve as foot soldiers in the ground war in Iraq and Syria. For example, it was hundreds of Muslim fighters who were killed on the ground in May 2016 in an effort to drive ISIS out from Raqqa, the group's major stronghold in Syria. And it was Muslim Peshmerga Kurdish fighters and the Muslim Iraqi forces that were dying on the battlefield in efforts to take back Mosul from ISIS during November of 2016. As CNN's Nick Payton Walsh reported from the war front, these Muslim soldiers were laying down their lives to defeat ISIS "on behalf of the world."

Beyond poverty, ethnic animosity and sectarian religious strife, the other key root cause of war (i.e., the deadly combination of gender inequality and male fantasy) also fuels terrorism in a variety of ways. First, joining a terrorist cause is a way for young men to show their worth as warriors and to live up to the "Boy Code" by which they have been brought up. Second, recruiters always promise "wives" and/or sex slaves in this world and virgins in heaven. Thus, joining a terror group, in addition to imparting meaning and purpose to a climactically violent masculine act, promises an endless fulfillment of these alienated young men's frustrated desire for conquest over women as sexual objects.

It is clear, therefore, that the root causes of war identified in this book (i.e., economic deprivation, racism, nationalism, religious strife and gender inequality) all play a role in the phenomenon of terrorism. In order to effectively eliminate the kind of radicalization that breeds easy recruits for terrorist masterminds, we must understand and address these root causes. Direct military intervention has been, and will continue to be, an ineffective response. Bombing terrorist strongholds may provide short-term treatments, such as pushing ISIS back from certain territories in Iraq or Syria. It will not, however, provide a solution to eliminating terrorism itself. It will simply continue to force this complex cancerous phenomenon to morph into new strains and to manifest itself in new places.

The days of brute force being a remedy to anything have come to an end in the twenty-first century.

We must go beyond the "War on Terror" and expand our toolbox for addressing this destructive trend. Not only has military force never been able to solve any of humanity's problems, increasingly, it has proven itself to be incapable of producing a winner.

In order to eliminate terrorism, including attacks by lone wolf terrorists on soft targets, we have no choice but to do the hard work of addressing the root causes of radicalization and war with long-term and effective solutions.

# Part 4: Ineffective Approaches to Peacekeeping and Security

A primary thesis of this book is that, in addition to the devastating human cost of military intervention, direct use of force has lost its power and effectiveness in reaching any of the security goals facing humanity in the twenty-first century. This includes defeating terrorism. In order to reach a lasting peace, we need to work to eliminate the root causes of war by becoming a catalyst in the constructive process. Facilitating and accelerating the maturation of the constructive process takes vision and long-term commitment and requires development and activation of new capacities, at both the systemic and individual levels.

To engage as a catalyst in the constructive process, we first need to gain a deeper understanding of the reasons for the increasing ineffectiveness of the largely palliative approaches to national security that have taken up the attention and resources of the world's nations in the past. These approaches, which incorporate elements of the destructive order, have been rendered obsolete in the twenty-first century. Nevertheless, they continue to have a hold on the imagination of foreign policy elites. Among these obsolescent approaches are paradigms that continue to advocate the involvement of the world's super-powers as balancers of worldwide military power and keepers of peace among nations.

Among examples of these outworn paradigms have been "Pax Britannica" during the nineteenth century, "Pax Americana" during the first half of the twentieth century and the balance of power main-tained during the cold war between the United States and the Union of Soviet Socialist Republics in the context of a nuclear arms race that threatened a Mu-tual Assured Destruction (MAD) if either of them launched a first strike.

It would be useful at this juncture to present a more detailed examination of the concepts of balance of power and "Pax Americana," both of which have comprised the primary approaches to global security during the last century.

Simply explained, the balance of power argu-ment holds that an equality of military strength be-tween individual states or groups of allied states is a fundamental prerequisite for preventing an outbreak of war. This argument rests on the assumption that all states are motivated by a desire to achieve suprema-cy over other countries, but would not attempt to do so at the risk of their own survival.

Even if we credit the balance of power paradigm with having prevented war for brief periods during the last two centuries, such a balancing act has always been a precarious concept on which to pin the future peace and prosperity of the world. In addition to being anchored in mutual fear, the balance of power approach suffers from a number of logical and practical inconsistencies. For example, the balance of power approach assumes perfect rationality in decisions made by nations to engage in armed conflict. It assumes that, before going to war, countries evaluate the enemy capabilities and make a rational decision based on their chances of victory. This is an unrealistic assumption, however, because rational calculations are only one factor among the many competing considerations that often shape a nation's collective, or a dictator's individual, decision to go to war. Indeed, more often than not, it is nationalistic hatreds, racial animosities and religious conflicts that drive nations into war, not level-headed and precise calculations of chances of victory. In such cases, facing an army of equal strength often does little to prevent war. In fact, even an army of far superior power cannot always persuade a weaker nation to avoid military conflict. This was clearly demonstrated during the Gulf crisis of the early 1990s, when the combined military might of such decidedly superior powers as the United States, Britain and France failed to prevent Saddam Hussein from forging ahead with a war he could not possibly win.

As a conceptual fraternal twin of the balance of power paradigm, the vision of the United States as the primary superpower in charge of keeping peace around the globe (i.e., a Pax Americana) continues to hold sway among some American think tanks and foreign policy elites. A Pax Americana is defined as a peaceful world order created and maintained under the leadership of the United States using a variety of options, including direct military intervention. Under such a system, the United States draws up the rules, decides which cases of aggression require a response and organizes a coalition to deliver it. At its heart, a Pax Americana is an authoritarian system of world leadership. True to authoritarian theory, it places great faith in the goodness, wisdom and justice of the United States and presumes it to have both the ability and the moral authority to promote the good of humanity as a whole.

Despite the continuing appeal of this vision in some American circles, the historical record of its pursuit has shown it to have all of the flaws of an authoritarian system. First, as may be expected, since America's rise to superpower status in the twentieth century, its world policing and intervention efforts have been mobilized, not on the basis of consistent ethical and humanitarian considerations, but primarily on the basis of whether the situation posed a present or potential danger to American interests. The fact that the United States turned away the *St. Louis*, a ship carrying Jewish refugees fleeing the Nazi assault in Europe and took no stand against Hitler's ominous advances until his Japanese allies attacked Pearl Harbor, provides a conspicuous example of the primacy of US national interests within any Pax Americana paradigm.

This inevitable—and many would argue, natural—tendency on the part of the United States to judge all situations with the yardstick of its own interests, has led much of the rest of the world to view the United States as lacking in the moral authority required to act as a credible protector of world peace.

Aside from the lopsided emphasis on US interests, another problem with any lingering quest for a Pax Americana is that it imposes a great economic burden on the United States, a burden that has already taken a great toll on American society. Given the country's economic conditions, it is questionable whether the United States, even if willing, would be able to continue its world policing efforts.

Thus, as approaches to security developed within the destructive plane, direct military intervention, balance of power and Pax Americana not only have exacerbated the wasteful expenditure of resources on military buildup among all nations—including those that have either acquired nuclear capability (e.g., India and Pakistan) or are vying to do so (e.g., Iran and North Korea)—they have proven ineffective in preventing war.

An important reason for the practical ineffectiveness of these approaches is that they reflect outworn mindsets rooted in delegitimized relationships of domination and subjugation based on military power. They are not only unable to address the root causes of war, but, at best, they represent increasingly barren means of treating the symptoms of conflict among nations.

Clearly, no one nation in the world is able to combine the ethical integrity, moral authority and economic capability needed to singlehandedly enforce peace across the globe. Ultimately, it is a democratic international system representing the interests of all humankind, not a dictatorial system based on the interests of one or more powerful nations, that can help humanity chart its path toward a lasting peace.

# Part 5: Facilitating the Constructive Process

So far in this book, we have taken stock of the constructive innovations and social transformations that have taken place in the world at an increasingly accelerated pace as a result of the discovery of new spiritual truths in the nineteenth century. We have also reviewed how this constructive process is challenging the outworn mindsets and practices that continue to inflict suffering on the human race.

Despite the robust forward movement of the constructive process, however, each of us still has a role to play in accelerating its fruition, at both the systemic and individual levels. The primary locus of the constructive process resides within the global consciousness of individuals who view themselves as members of one interconnected human family, and it is this collective consciousness that needs to be acted upon to fuel the growth and maturation of an international system capable of serving the global public good.

In this chapter, I will outline a vision for the evolution of the constructive process at both the systemic and individual levels.

## The System

The embryo of a constructive international system already exists in the collection of the global agencies that comprise the United Nations and other supranational collaborative bodies that seek to operate on the basis of shared interests that transcend racial, national, religious and economic boundaries. This embryonic system, however, exists as an unfulfilled potential and needs to evolve into a unified federation of nations capable of promoting and safeguarding a peaceful global order.

One of the major stepping-stones toward a mature system of international collaboration is collective security. This principle is already enshrined in the UN Charter, but is yet to be fully implemented. Collective security envisions an international peace-keeping system based on the commitment of all nations to rise collectively against aggression and to exert all types of pressures, including moral, diplomatic, economic and military, to frustrate any attack by one state against another. As the system matures, political and economic sanctions are expected to act as increasingly powerful deterrents, obviating the need for collective military action. In a system of collective security, there is no place for case-by-case calculations of self-interest by each country before joining in collective action against aggression. Rather, the proper functioning of the system requires that all countries enter into a binding commitment, identify their national interests with the preservation of the total world order and consider the threat of aggression anywhere as a threat to their own interests.

The first international attempt at establishing a collective security system was made at the end of the First World War by the American President, Woodrow Wilson. Wary of the horrors of the war, President Wilson proposed the establishment of an international structure (i.e., a League of Nations) charged with the task of ensuring world peace on the basis of a collective security system. Despite the league's formal establishment in 1920, President Wilson's failure to persuade the US Congress to endorse American membership in the league, coupled with the international conflicts still brewing in the war's aftermath, prevented the League of Nations from achieving its mission.

Although the League of Nations failed to put a system of collective security into operation, the international debate leading to its establishment infused the concept with enough credibility for it to be later incorporated in the charter of the United Nations. Yet, despite the great emphasis placed on collective security in the UN charter, the United Nation's ability to enforce the system has been seriously curtailed by the veto power given to the permanent members of the UN Security Council. The veto power provision, in effect, makes it impossible to enforce collective security action against the permanent members presiding over the council. As a result, the UN's collective security provisions, subject as they are to deliberation by the Security Council, can only be enforced against less powerful states, or against states not backed by the veto power of a permanent member.

Many of the wars and atrocities of the twenty-first century, including those that followed the use of chemical weapons and, later, the indiscriminate bombing of hundreds of innocent civilian men, women and children in Aleppo by Syrian President, Bashar-al-Assad (an ally of Russia, which is a permanent Security Council member), could have been prevented by a true system of collective security. Within a collective security system, political leaders who commit "crimes against humanity" would be apprehended and put on trial by the International Criminal Court, obviating the perceived need by the superpowers to engage in direct military attacks and/ or proxy wars that result in the killing or displacement of millions of innocent people in the process.

The implementation of a true system of collective security is also a prerequisite for initiating a gradual reduction in the stockpiles of weapons around the globe. Under a collective security system, the UN peacekeeping forces would be empowered to maintain order, while a globally unified regime of economic and diplomatic sanctions would function as the primary means of preventing aggression.

The full implementation of collective security is, thus, one of the major systemic transformations required in the forward movement of the constructive process. Among other benefits, the economic dividends of a well-established system of collective security would be of such a scale so as to facilitate the alleviation of many destabilizing conditions in the world, including poverty. According to an estimate by Oxfam, it would cost a mere sixty billion dollars to eradicate poverty throughout the world. That is less than the cost of two-dozen American B2-Spirit bombers and a negligible fraction of the multi-trillion-dollar annual military budget of the world's 196 sovereign nations.

The ultimate removal of the veto power from the permanent members of the UN Security Council and the implementation of a true collective security system require meeting a number of milestones in international relations along the way. This includes the achievement of a level of political unification that would allow for substantial reductions in the level of mutual threats among nations. Such a growth in the levels of regional and international cooperation is also a prerequisite for achieving meaningful reductions in the stockpiles of nuclear weapons, an objective that has long held the center stage in the peace process pursued by a variety of international organizations, visionary politicians and grassroots peace movements.

During the latter part of the twentieth century, a number of steps were taken toward reducing nuclear stockpiles. The United Nations Nuclear Non-proliferation Treaty took effect in 1970 and, since then, a total of 191 countries have joined the treaty. Concurrently, the world has witnessed the rise of a culture of "nuclear taboo" and even an international movement by several former and current world leaders toward a "Global Zero," which advocates for the elimination of nuclear weapons among all nations in the world. These are advances that must, indeed, be celebrated. Yet, as important as these efforts have been, history provides evidence that the production of weapons is primarily a symptom rather than a cause of conflict. Nations have tended to expand their armaments either when they have been threatened or when they have intended to invade or subdue other countries. Similarly, a reduction in the level of conflict and the prevalence of peaceful relations among nations has often resulted in reductions in the level of armaments. For a clear illustration of this fact, we need to look no further than to the history of the nuclear arms race itself.

Throughout the course of the arms race between the United States and the former Soviet Union, efforts toward nuclear arms control were pursued not only within the United Nations, but also in the context of bilateral negotiations between the two countries. As may be expected, however, in the absence of a fundamental resolution of conflicts, these negotiations achieved little in the way of meaningful reductions in the nuclear arsenals. Even the growing grass-roots nuclear disarmament movements, such as the Nuclear Freeze movement in the United States and the Green Peace movement in Western Europe, though successful in capturing world attention, appeared unable to substantially influence the course of the arms race. It was not until the late 1980s, when major political changes in the Soviet Union and the warming of the relationship between Presidents Gorbachev and Reagan helped reduce the level of tension between the two superpowers that the first major reductions in nuclear arsenals were achieved. Thus, the history of the arms race not only confirms the nature of nuclear arms production as a symptom of conflict, but it also suggests that the only logical path to an ultimate nuclear disarmament is continuing improvement in international relations.

Even if it were possible to impose an international ban on nuclear production by all countries, including the Third World countries that possess such weapons, this by itself would do little to facilitate world peace. Just as treating the symptoms of a disease will not eliminate the disease itself, banning nuclear weapons is unlikely to bring an end to war. Without first addressing the causes of conflict, eliminating nuclear weapons will not ensure that the resources previously devoted to their production will not be used to produce other devastating weapons. Indeed, if it were even possible to eliminate all types and classes of weapons from the face of the earth, this would still not guarantee an end to war. People are ingenious enough to invent other forms of warfare to kill large numbers of innocent people.

Let us not forget that while two hundred thousand people were killed in the aftermath of the two atomic bombs that were dropped on Hiroshima and Nagasaki in 1945, over eight hundred thousand people were slaughtered during the 1994 genocide in Rwanda using hand-held machetes.

Therefore, any effort to rid humanity from the threat of nuclear weapons, including the danger posed by their potential use by terrorists and the tremendous economic waste and environmental devastation involved in the process of their production, can only succeed by working within the constructive process to strengthen the bonds of international friendship and trust.

In addition to the removal of the veto power and implementation of collective security, the United Nation's evolution as an international system of collaboration capable of facilitating the constructive process requires it to not only achieve, but also surpass the goal of becoming a democratic body. In its current definition, "democracy" allows for equal representation in what is often an adversarial decision-making process. In the evolving constructive international system, the decision-making process itself needs to go beyond debates representing the interests of specific member-states, to consultation on solutions that benefit humanity as a whole.

In this new model for collective decision-making, representatives of people from diverse backgrounds, viewpoints and beliefs would come together, not to engage in debates designed to win a preconceived argument, but to use their right to free expression to consult and reach the best solution for all.

Recent collective international efforts, including the historic 2015 agreement in Paris to mitigate climate change, indicate that the constructive process is moving the UN member-states forward toward adopting precisely such a consultative model.

The maturation of the international system toward becoming a consultative and collaborative federation of nations, protected by a fully implemented system of collective security, requires a change in the individual mindset and an ultimate transformation in the existing relationships among human beings. A unified international system requires the achievement of unity among people of diverse backgrounds.

## The Individual

In order to enable the emerging structures of supranational collaboration to chart a clear path toward a lasting peace, we must first achieve a fundamental change in the relationships among human beings based on a global sense of belonging. It is this sense of belonging—a critical choice between an "exclusive" or "inclusive" identity—that holds the ultimate key to a lasting peace.

Such a transformation is, in fact, well within reach. The history of civilization abounds with evidence that human beings are fully capable of expanding their sense of identity. That has been the case with the successive expansions of the primary unit of identity from the family, to the village, to the tribe, to the city-state and to the nation. At this juncture in human history we do not need to look far to see that, increasingly, the primary unit of identity for the younger generation around the world is the global society and realize that the truth of oneness of humanity is already part and parcel of the constructive collective consciousness in the twenty-first century.

Oneness of humanity is the scientific and spiritual truth that animates the spirit of our age. Thus, all we need to do as catalysts in the constructive process is to align ourselves with this spirit and work to build model communities that reflect its constructive attributes of racial, national and religious harmony, gender equality and economic equity.

In that context, the work of a catalyst in the constructive process differs markedly from the political activism that has long been upheld as the primary means of effecting positive social change. As catalysts in the constructive process, we do not need to "fight against" anything. The destructive mindsets and institutions of the past are collapsing ever more visibly under their own weight all around us, similar to a wooden structure that has been eaten through by termites. They are tottering and crumbling. Our task, therefore, is not to engage in fighting the destructive process, but rather to gently beckon those who are caught up in these destructive mindsets and structures to join us in building new communities and relationships within the constructive plane.

Being caught up in the destructive plane is particularly unsettling and painful at this point in human history because it is a realm of palpable fear. The privileges it stood for are slipping away, and the values it upheld have been challenged and delegitimized. In this realm, some have lost hope, while others are fighting to turn back the clock.

The distressful condition of those who are still caught up in the destructive mindset is analogous to that of people flying in an old and dilapidated airplane that is bumping up and down in severe turbulence and threatening to fall apart and crash at any given moment. In this drama, a few people are in deep sleep, many are trembling in fear and others are desperately thinking about how to save the plane from impending crash. In this analogy, the constructive process may be likened to a state-of-the-art airplane, moving at the appropriate altitude and speed toward its destination. In addition to being safe and reliable, this plane features a sky-bridge that can be hooked up to the old plane, allowing its distressed and fearful passengers to walk over to the new plane. As catalysts in the constructive process, all we need to do is to roll out the bridge and beckon and encourage those riding in the old plane to join us. If we do so lovingly, we can be hopeful that many of them will join us voluntarily. But we must remain cognizant of the fact that there are bound to be some passengers in the old plane not yet courageous enough to leave their familiar, though turbulent, environment.

The reluctance of the people who are struggling within the destructive process to step into the constructive plane may be the result of many different individual factors. There is little doubt, however, that, at the collective level, a major barrier to alignment with the constructive consciousness is a conspicuous paralysis of will, fueled by a generalized belief in the incorrigibly aggressive nature of human beings and a view of the world that continues to be informed by win-lose scenarios. This erroneous notion, combined with the hopelessness and cynicism generated by the ongoing tumult in the destructive plane, continues to prevent many people from even attempting to become facilitators of constructive change. In order to generate hope and faith among people of all mindsets and backgrounds for the future of humanity, we must first empirically and scientifically refute the assertion that human beings are aggressive by nature.

A careful investigation of the empirical data produced by twenty-first century science, encompassing psychology, anthropology and genetics, shows a preponderance of evidence that collaboration, not aggression, has been the key to our evolution and survival as a human species. Today, we know that human beings are not ruled by their DNA. Rather, changes in the environment can lead to changes in the DNA of human beings. In essence, the science of the twenty-first century has now squarely rejected the fatalism of an inescapably aggressive nature in favor of a malleable human nature, highly responsive not only to its baser instincts, but also to its "better angels."

Important new research, furthermore, has produced unequivocal evidence that human beings are motivated, first and foremost, by a desire for comradery and love. Among these studies, the work of Sebastian Junger, best-selling author and war journalist, is of special interest. Junger, who has lived alongside soldiers and reported from war zones for over twenty years, grew curious to know why most soldiers who return home from war miss the war. At first, Junger found this phenomenon (i.e., the soldiers' yearning to return to the battlefield) quite unbelievable given the fact that there is nothing attractive about being in a war zone. As Junger states, there is no running water, no electricity, no cooked food, no TV and no Internet; and each soldier is constantly facing the threat of being maimed or killed. Junger also knew that these soldiers were not crazy; they neither enjoyed killing, nor being killed. So, why did they miss being at war after they returned home?

Investigating this issue more deeply, Junger discovered that the young men who are part of a brigade almost always develop a very close bond with their fellow soldiers; they find a deep emotional connection of comradery and brotherhood and a kind of love that says, "Don't worry brother. I have your back. I will protect you even if I have to sacrifice my own life." In other words, while they are in the trenches of war, they experience the kind of deep connection and love they have always yearned for as human beings. It is this experience of unconditional love that causes them to miss being at war.

In his best-selling book, *Tribe: On Homecoming and Belonging* (2016), Junger produces further evidence of how this sense of mutual connection and comradery has been shown to be a major predictor of human happiness. He provides evidence, for example, of how the self-reported levels of happiness among Londoners increased during the intense period of German bombing of London and its surroundings (the "Blitz") during WWII, as people came together to support each other at a time of shared adversity. Junger, however, stops short of taking these findings to their logical conclusion in his book, perhaps reflecting the generalized paralysis of will. In line with the arguments in his book, and in response to a question during a 2016 interview on NPR about what his findings might imply for changes that can make the world a better place, Junger nostalgically harkened back to the close-knit small towns of the past as the preferred model for social organization.

But, while it is true that, historically, human beings have primarily had the opportunity to experience the bliss of comradery in small towns and "exclusive" environments, it does not necessarily follow that we can only experience the joy of being valued, loved and cared for in small and exclusive "tribal" units. Comradery can happen in two ways: it can happen when we love "exclusively," or when we love "inclusively." Both conditions can create the bliss of connectedness we all seek as human beings. The difference is that one belongs to the destructive plane, and the other resides within the constructive consciousness. As such, our task as catalysts in the constructive process is to facilitate a transition from an "exclusive" to an "inclusive" identity throughout human society based on the recognition of the truth of oneness of humanity.

In addition to its status as the primary foundation of spirituality, oneness of humanity is a fact for which the science of the twenty-first century has provided solid empirical evidence. Today, based on DNA tracking, we know that all human beings started in the same geographic area of the planet in Africa fifty to eighty thousand years ago. Later, as different groups of people moved to different parts of the world, they adjusted to different living conditions and climates and began to differentiate in their physical appearance and skin color. As such, science has now produced unequivocal evidence that there is only one race—the human race.

Thus, we live at a time in human history when both the spiritual and scientific truths required for a new and complete transformation in social consciousness and relationships have already been revealed to humanity. For the first time in history, science has become an ally of spirituality.

The convergence of science and spirituality on the principle of oneness of humanity has prepared the way for us to educate and empower the younger generation to independently investigate the truth and join us as catalysts in the constructive plane, voluntarily and of their own accord.

By about age eleven or twelve, every young person in the world is engaged in an intensive search for identity. She or he is yearning for love and acceptance, often expressed as "fitting in." More so than people of any other age, young adolescents stand at a critical juncture and must make a choice—will they step into the constructive or the destructive plane? Will they turn into potential terrorists, gang members and mass shooters, or will they become the builders of a better world? Will they follow a new generation of power-mongers and fall for their divide-and-conquer tactics, or will they have the discernment to see through the falsehood and devastation of such plots? Terrorist groups, gangs and even school cliques, are all examples of "exclusive" groups that beckon young people in their search for identity and acceptance, and the outcome for each young person depends largely on whether she/he is empowered to find comradery in inclusive environments or is left alone to retreat into exclusive groups.

As many people who have worked with the younger generation throughout the world have observed, members of the new generation in the twenty-first century are fully prepared to expand the limits of their sense of identity. As the most globally connected human generation ever, they espouse a global sense of belonging and are ready to build model communities that are inclusive, unified and peaceful. Our job is simply to empower them and to gently accompany them into the constructive plane.

In addition to upholding the truth of oneness of humanity, a key aspect of facilitating a transition to a constructive global consciousness is educating young boys and girls in gender equality. Removing the "Boy Code" from the upbringing of boys and allowing them to express their emotions within loving and constructive environments are vital to a robust peace education. Violent masculinity, a relic of the destructive mindset, needs to be replaced by a strong sense of empowerment to build peaceful communities.

## Whence the Global Culture?

When we speak about international collaboration to build a unified and peaceful world, important questions arise that must be answered. What kind of global culture is likely to emerge in such a world? Does unity mean uniformity? And, will it require the dissolution of diverse cultures into a homogeneous product, most likely representing the dominant western cultural values?

Unity among diverse peoples and nations does not, in any way, require that human beings lose their cultural diversity. In fact, the constructive evolution in human relationships must ensure the preservation and celebration of cultural diversity. Unification can only provide its highest benefit to humanity when we succeed in upholding equal respect and dignity for all members of the human race, while maintaining the diversity of human cultural heritage.

Treading a constructive path toward achieving unity in diversity is not only vital for facilitating the realization of a peaceful world, but it is required for enabling humanity to reach new frontiers of cultural and scientific progress. It is only through preserving our diversity that we can achieve two of the most important prerequisites for a constructive global culture—balance and creativity.

The vital importance of balance arises from the fact that every characteristic, whether individual or collective, reaches its highest good when it manifests itself in moderation, and it becomes harmful and negative when taken to an extreme.

In order for the global culture to evolve into its richest and most beneficial form, therefore, all of the different cultures in the world would need to be able to participate in shaping it. It is only through such a mutual give and take that a rich and balanced culture can be brought into being in the global society.

When any culture remains inward looking and isolated, many of the characteristics of that culture that could be a source of strength and progress in moderation tend to be taken to an extreme and, thus, yield negative results in the lives of the people of that culture.

For example, one of the characteristics of the Japanese culture—within which I lived for a total of four years—is "group-orientation." In the Japanese culture, people are discouraged from speaking their minds and showing their individuality, and each individual feels obligated to conform to and abide by the will of the group at all times. There is a saying in Japan that, "The nail that stands out gets hammered."

During the years that I lived in that beautiful country, I witnessed how such a positive characteristic (i.e., respecting the needs of the group) could be turned into a negative force in the lives of individuals and society when taken to an extreme. One of the examples of this negative manifestation was a scene that I witnessed every evening on the trains, in which Japanese "salary men" (company employees) would be returning to their families after drinking for a few hours in bars, in a state of complete inebriation. Upon inquiring about it, I was told that getting drunk is the only way they are able to speak their minds and share their true feelings.

On the opposite pole is "individualism," which is a key characteristic of the American culture. Just like "group orientation," which strengthens collaboration, "individualism" can also play a very positive role in the lives of human beings; for example, by aiding personal development and independence of thought and action. However, if individualism is taken to an extreme, it too can change from a foundation for independence and intellectual growth to become a cause of self-centeredness, egotism and ruthless competition in all aspects of life.

All cultures in the world, therefore, need the many different characteristics reflected in the world's diverse cultures in balance; a balance that can only be achieved through mutual exchange, learning and cooperation.

Achieving unity in diversity is also a prerequisite for ensuring optimum creativity in every area of human activity. Recent studies in a wide range of fields, from business management to technological innovation, have confirmed this fact. Studies have shown, for example, that when a diverse group of employees collaborate to find a solution to a problem while being given equal opportunity to express their ideas freely, they are far more creative and productive than a group of people from the same background.

The vital importance of unity in diversity as a key feature of the constructive process should not be surprising. Unity in diversity is the foundation of life. As the science of ecological biology has clearly shown, every living system in the world, including the human body, owes its growth and sustainability to the variety and diversity of the elements in its environment. In fact, the human body is, at once, the most diverse and the most unified system in all of creation. The cells comprising the heart are very different from those making up the brain. In the same way, the cells in all other subsystems and organs are distinctly unique and different from each other. Yet, all of them collaborate in harmony to sustain life in the body.

Unity in diversity is also a feature of the totality of the universe. Despite the amazing variety in the shapes and colors of minerals, plants and animals on our planet and the vastness and diversity reflected in the billions of galaxies in the cosmos, an inherent unity is visible at all levels of the universe, from the sub-atomic to the macro-cosmic. In between the micro and the macro, fractal patterns repeat themselves with amazing mathematical precision throughout the universe. The law of unity in diversity is the primary formula of life, both physical and spiritual.

# Conclusion

Despite the rapid process of disintegration visible all around us, there is a new spirit of awakening propelling us toward a peaceful world. As creative individuals with unique talents and capabilities, we each hold the power to become a catalyst within this constructive process. Ultimately, the achievement of a lasting peace depends upon unified collaboration among a critical mass of individuals committed to building inclusive, loving and harmonious communities. It is only through such a collaborative effort among diverse people that the embryonic global system can acquire the spirit of unity required for its successful evolution into a federation of nations capable of serving the global public good.

In closing, I offer the following poem, which I wrote shortly before starting this book, as a gift to every enlightened soul.

*If God had deemed it sufficient to create only one color,*

*And if He had created only one note,*
*And if He had gifted us with only one*
*flower,*
*Exquisite paintings, magnificent harmo-*
*nies, and celestial gardens*
*Would have been sacrificed.*

*When He breathed the spirit of life into*
*humanity,*
*He fashioned a pattern of unity out of*
*diversity.*
*So that the creative capacity of His crea-*
*tures would remain endless,*
*He wove the tapestry of life out of many*
*colors and variations.*

*The secret of true knowledge and adora-*
*tion of the Beloved is love; that is all.*
*Infinite and inclusive love; love of enemy;*
*love of friend.*
*The oneness of humanity is not a dream;*
*it is the very essence of creation.*
*It is reflected in our physical body; it is*
*the source of life in each breath.*

*To remember the secret of our existence,*
*let us ponder how in this body*
*The red heart beats for the white brain.*
*A tear has the same crystal color of pu-*
*rity, whether the eyes are green, blue, or*
*black.*

*As the creator has done, let us endeavor to do my friends.*

# About the Author

Dr. Roya Akhavan currently serves as Professor and Director of Graduate Studies at the Department of Mass Communications, St. Cloud State University. She is an award-winning educator and scholar, whose research has been published in top international peer-reviewed journals. Dr. Akhavan's work in the field of mass communication extends into a wide range of related areas, including international affairs, peace studies, gender issues, and spirituality in the 21st century. She is a frequent speaker at national and international forums and radio and television programs.

Dr. Akhavan has lived and worked in four different cultures: Persian, American, Japanese, and Chinese. She currently lives in Minneapolis, Minnesota.

Made in the USA
Lexington, KY
24 September 2018